HOW TO BE RICH

HOW
TO BE
RICH

by
J. Paul Getty

A PLAYBOY PRESS BOOK

CONTENTS

PREFACE

In 1960, the editors of PLAYBOY magazine approached me with a request that I prepare a series of articles based on the theme: "Men, Money and Values in Today's Society."

Admittedly, I found the proposal flattering—as who would not? On the other hand, I seriously questioned my qualifications for the task. My entire adult life had been devoted to building and operating business enterprises. I doubted that this experience equipped me to hold forth on a variety of subjects before an audience of millions.

Besides, I was—and, for that matter, still am—active in business. I was far from certain that I would have the time necessary to write. Finally, I wasn't at all convinced that the magazine's readers would be very interested in what I had to say.

But my doubts and reservations were overcome by what, to me, seemed valid and convincing considerations and arguments.

First of all, I had long been aware that American business and businessmen and the entire free-enterprise system were very often the targets of severe criticism—and even abuse. Few, indeed, were the reasoned replies and rebuttals which reached the eyes and ears of the general public.

Preface

Then, as I—and so many other successful businessmen of my acquaintance—have so frequently noted, many young people today enter upon business careers without sufficient grounding and preparation. By this, I do not mean that they lack specialized training. Rather, it is that they fail to grasp the over-all, the long-range picture. They do not understand and appreciate the universally applicable fundamentals, the basic philosophies, the endless implications and ramifications —and particularly the numberless responsibilities—which are the absolute essentials of business in this complex age.

Also—and this was far from the least of the considerations which decided me—I felt that, in our contemporary society, far too much emphasis was being placed on *getting* rich, on amassing wealth. Little if any attention was being paid to the very important question of *how to be rich,* how to discharge the responsibilities created by wealth even while constructively enjoying the privileges and prerogatives conferred by it.

After all, "richness" is at least as much a matter of character, of philosophy, outlook and attitude, as it is of money. The "millionaire mentality" is not—and in this day and age, cannot be—merely an accumulative mentality. The able, ambitious man who strives for success must understand that the term "rich" has infinite shadings of meaning. In order to justify himself and his wealth, he must know *how to be rich* in virtually every positive sense of the term.

These factors—and some others—all contributed to my final decision to accede to the editors' request.

I might add that PLAYBOY's Editor-Publisher, Hugh M. Hefner, and the magazine's Editorial Director, A. C. Spectorsky, promised that I would be granted carte blanche to say what I wanted, regardless of how unconventional, nonconformist or controversial my views happened to be. They have kept this promise faithfully through the ensuing years —but I am getting ahead of myself.

"I will prepare the first piece, and then we'll see," I said, in effect.

The results, to say the least, were surprising to me. Although what I have written is unconventional, even iconoclastic, the response has been overwhelmingly favorable. Evidently, many people shared my views or had been waiting for someone to express opinions confirming their own deep-seated doubts and unease about widely accepted doctrines and theories.

It has been a source of immeasurable satisfaction that my writing for PLAYBOY has been well received, widely quoted and has inspired thousands of favorable comments and letters from press and public. This book is the result of that reception.

In the years that have intervened since the first article was published, I have often been asked three questions—questions I would like to answer here as simply and directly as possible.

1. Why, considering the large number of magazines being published in America today, did I choose PLAYBOY as the medium through which to express my views?

The answer is, indeed, simple. PLAYBOY enjoys a very high readership among young executives and college students. These are the individuals who will be the businessmen and business leaders of the future. These are precisely the individuals who would be likely to benefit from any information I might impart as a result of my own experience in the business world. These are the young men, and women, whose thinking processes can—and should—be prodded by ideas and opinions not necessarily contained in textbooks or staid, overconservative publications. Whether they accept or reject the ideas is immaterial; they are able to think, and they *do* think constructively as a result of mental stimuli. They are, in short, the individuals to whom I want to address any "message" I can offer.

2. Why did I want to express my views in the first place?

I have already touched on this, but I feel that some amplification might be in order. I've said that although business is often attacked publicly, it does not very often find many public defenders. The average businessman generally speaks before board or stockholders' meetings or at trade-association, Chamber of Commerce or service-club luncheons and dinners. When he writes, it is usually for house organs or trade journals. Although he has a very vital and important message for the public at large, he seldom receives, or takes, the opportunity to deliver it. Simply stated, I have tried to start the ball rolling —and I hope that I may have encouraged other successful businessmen to air their views before the general public.

3. What do I hope to achieve by my writing?

Beyond what I have already mentioned, I have several hopes and aims. I would like to convince young businessmen that there are no sure-fire, quick-and-easy formulas for success in business, that there are no ways in which a man can automatically become a millionaire in business.

There are no tricks, no magical incantations or sorcerer's potions which can make a business or a businessman an overnight success. Many qualities and much hard work are needed, as are innumerable other elements, before a businessman or woman can achieve success and reach the millionaire level. The various qualities, elements and factors which other successful businessmen and I have found to be essential or helpful are subjects of this book.

I am firmly convinced that the future of American business, of the American people—and, indeed, of the entire free world —lies in the perpetuation of a progressive, farsighted free-enterprise system guided by progressive, farsighted businessmen who will reap their rewards from improving the living standards of all. If, by writing this book, I have passed this message on—even if only to a receptive few—then I shall have achieved my purpose and received a very rich reward in the form of personal gratification from the thought that I have in some small measure helped spread and strengthen the principles in which I believe.

—J. Paul Getty

PART ONE

Becoming a Millionaire

HOW
I MADE
MY FIRST BILLION

Though this book is not an autobiography, the views I express in it are my own and have grown out of my life experience. I think, therefore, that a brief description of my career might be of interest to the reader. If I have a business "philosophy," it was formed in the oil fields and elsewhere in the oil industry.

After many fruitless months of prospecting for oil in Oklahoma, I finally spudded my first test well not far from Stone Bluff, a tiny Muskogee County hamlet, in early January 1916.

On February 2, the bailer—the device which cleared formation rock from the drill hole—brought up a quantity of oil sand. This indicated that we were nearing the final stages of drilling; the next 24 hours would prove whether the well was a producer or a dry hole.

I was still very young and quite green. My nervousness and excitement rose to an intolerable pitch. I became more hindrance than help to the men on my drilling crew. To get out of their way and ease my own tension, I beat a strategic retreat to Tulsa, the nearest city of any size. I decided to wait there until the drilling operation was completed and the results were known. In Tulsa, J. Carl Smith, a close friend who was considerably older and far less excitable than I, volunteered to go to the drilling site and supervise the work there for me.

There were no telephones in the remote area where my well was being drilled. The single line between Stone Bluff and Tulsa seldom worked. Hence, J. Carl Smith promised to return to Tulsa on the last train from Stone Bluff the next day and inform me of the latest developments.

On the following day, I was at the Tulsa railroad depot, anxiously pacing the windswept passenger platform more than an hour before the train was due to arrive. At last, it pulled into the station. Endless seconds later, J. Carl Smith's familiar figure emerged from one of the coaches. His face beamed, and my hopes soared.

"Congratulations, Paul!" he boomed when he saw me on the platform. "We brought in your well this afternoon. It's producing thirty barrels!"

I automatically assumed he meant thirty barrels a day, and my elation vanished instantly. Thirty barrels a day—why, that was a mere trickle compared to the gushers other oilmen were bringing in at the time.

"Yes, sir," J. Carl grinned. "We're getting thirty barrels an hour . . ."

Thirty barrels *an hour!*

That made a difference, a world of difference. That meant the well was producing 720 barrels of crude oil daily. It also meant that I was in the oil business—to stay.

As the son of a successful oilman, I had been exposed to the virus of oil fever since childhood. My parents, George F. and Sarah Getty, and I first visited what was then the Oklahoma Territory in 1903, when I was ten. While there, my father, a prosperous Minneapolis attorney-at-law, found it impossible to resist the lure of the Oklahoma Oil Rush, which was then in full swing. He formed the Minnehoma Oil Company and began prospecting for oil.

My father, a self-made man who had known extreme poverty in his youth, had a practically limitless capacity for hard work, and he also had an almost uncanny talent for finding oil. After organizing Minnehoma Oil, he personally supervised the drilling of 43 oil wells, of which 42 proved to be producers!

I served a tough and valuable apprenticeship working as

a roustabout and tooldresser in the oil fields in 1910 and 1911, but I didn't go into the oil business for myself until September 1914. I had but recently returned to the United States after attending Oxford University in England for two years. My original intent was to enter the U.S. Diplomatic Service, but I deferred that plan in order to try my luck as an independent operator—a wildcatter—in Oklahoma.

The times were favorable. It was a bonanza era for the burgeoning American petroleum industry. A lusty, brawling pioneer spirit still prevailed in the oil fields. The Great Oil Rush continued with unabated vigor and was given added impetus by the war that had broken out in Europe that year. Primitive boomtowns dotted the Oklahoma countryside. Many bore bare-knuckled frontier-era names such as those of the four "Right" towns: Drumright, Dropright, Allright and Damnright.

Streets and roads were unpaved—rivers of mushy clay and mud in spring and winter and sun-baked, rutted tracks perpetually shrouded by billowing clouds of harsh red or yellow dust in summer. Duckboard sidewalks outside the more prosperous business establishments and gambling halls were viewed as the ultimate in civic improvements.

The atmosphere was identical to that which historians describe as prevailing in the California gold fields during the 1849 Gold Rush. In Oklahoma, the fever was to find oil, not gold, and it was an epidemic. There were few, indeed, who were immune to the contagion. Fortunes were being made—and lost—daily. It was not unusual for a penniless wildcatter, down to his last bit and without cash or credit with which to buy more, to drill another hundred feet and bring in a well that made him a rich man. A lease which sold for a few hundred dollars one afternoon sometimes increased in value a hundredfold or even a thousandfold by the next morning.

On the other hand, there were men who invested all they owned in leases and drilling operations only to find that they had nothing to show for their money and efforts but a few dismally dry holes. Leases purchased at peak prices one day proved to be utterly valueless the next. It was all a supremely thrilling gamble for staggering stakes, and I plunged into the whirl hopefully. I had no capital of my

3

own; my personal budget was $100 per month. My first year was anything but profitable. Large oil strikes were being reported regularly, and other wildcatters were bringing in gushers and big producers, but fortune seemed to elude me.

Then, in the late fall of 1915, a half-interest in an oil lease near Stone Bluff in Muskogee County—the Nancy Taylor Allotment—was offered for sale at public auction. I inspected the property and thought it highly promising. I knew other independent operators were interested in obtaining the lease, and this worried me. I didn't have much money at my disposal—certainly not enough to match the prices older, established oilmen would be able to offer. For this reason, I requested my bank to have one of its representatives bid for me at the sale without revealing my identity as the real bidder.

Surprisingly enough, this rather transparent stratagem accomplished the purpose I intended. The sale, held in the town of Muskogee—the county seat—was attended by several independent oil operators eager to obtain the lease. The unexpected appearance of the well-known bank executive who bid for me unnerved the wildcatters. They assumed that if a banker was present at the auction, it could only mean that some large oil company was also interested in the property and was prepared to top any and all offers. The independents glumly decided it would be futile to bid and, in the end, I secured the lease for $500—a bargain-basement price!

Soon thereafter, a corporation was formed to finance the drilling of a test well on the property. I, as a wildcatter with no capital of my own, received a modest 15-percent interest in the corporation. I assembled a crack drilling crew, and my men and I labored to erect the necessary wooden derrick and to rush the actual drilling operations. I remained on the site night and day until the drilling went into its final stages. Then, as I've related, I found it impossible to stand the nervous strain and fled to Tulsa, where my friend J. Carl Smith brought me the news that the well had come in.

The lease on the property was sold to a producing oil company two weeks after that, and I realized $12,000 as my share of the profits. The amount was not very impressive when compared to the huge sums others were making, but it was enough to convince me that I should—and would—remain in the oil business as a wildcatter.

My father and I had previously formed a partnership. Under its terms he was to provide financing for any exploration and drilling I conducted and supervised for the partnership. In return, he would receive 70 percent of the profits, while I received the remaining 30 percent. After my first success, we incorporated the partnership and in May 1916 formed the Getty Oil Company, in which I received a 30-percent stock interest.

Many fanciful—and entirely erroneous—accounts of the business relationship between us have appeared in print. Contrary to some published reports, my father did not set me up in business by giving me any outright cash gifts. George F. Getty rejected any ideas that a successful man's son should be pampered or spoiled or given money as a gift after he was old enough to earn his own living. My father *did* finance some of my early operations—but solely on the 70/30-percent basis. Insofar as lease purchases and drilling or other operations I conducted on my own account were concerned, I financed these myself. My father neither provided the money for my private business ventures nor did he share in the profits I received from them.

Incidentally, there is another popular misconception I'd like to correct once and for all. It has been said that my father bequeathed me a huge fortune when he passed away in 1930. Actually, he left me $500,000 in his will—a considerable sum, I'll admit, but nonetheless a very small part of his fortune. It was a token bequest. My father was well aware that I had already made several million dollars on my own, and he left the bulk of his estate to my mother.

After Father and I incorporated our partnership in 1916, I went right on prospecting and drilling for oil. My enthusiasm was not dampened when my second well proved to be a dry hole. By then, wildcatting was in my blood and I continued to buy and sell leases and to drill wells. I usually acted as my own geologist, legal advisor, drilling superintendent, explosives expert and even, on occasion, as roughneck and roustabout. The months that followed were extremely fortunate ones. In most instances, the leases I bought were sold at a profit, and when I drilled on a property, I struck oil more often than not.

There were no secrets, no mystical formulas behind these successes. I operated in much the same manner as did almost all wildcatters—with one important exception. In those days, the science of petroleum geology had not yet gained very wide acceptance in the oil fields. Many oilmen sneered openly at the idea that some "damned bookworm" could help them find oil. At best, the vast majority of oilmen were skeptical about geology as a practical science and put little stock in geologists' reports. I was among the few who believed in geology. I studied the subject avidly at every opportunity, and applied what I learned to my operations.

The independent operator had to possess a certain amount of basic knowledge and skill. He also needed reliable, loyal and experienced men on his exploration and drilling crews. But, beyond these things, I believe the most important factor that determined whether a wildcatter would succeed or fail— whether he would bring in a producing well or wind up with a dry hole—was just plain luck.

There were some who didn't consider it luck, among them T. N. Barnsdall, one of the great Oklahoma oil pioneers. Multimillionaire Barnsdall often expounded his favorite theory about what he thought made the difference.

"It's not luck," he maintained stoutly. "A man either has a nose for oil or he doesn't. If he does, he smells the stuff even when it's 3,000 feet down!"

Perhaps. But I rather doubt it myself. Personally, I was never able to sniff out the presence of a subterranean oil pool. Nor do I recall that I ever tingled with an oil dowser's extrasensory response while tramping across a potential drilling site. I still think my early successes were due mainly to pure luck.

However, lest there be those who imagine wildcatters had little to do but wait for the wheel of fortune to spin and then reap their profits, let me say that the oil business was never an easy one. It has always entailed work—hard work— and it has always been fraught with innumerable financial pitfalls, especially in the early days. Wells sometimes blew up, and profits—and often capital—were devoured with appalling speed by costly efforts to extinguish the resulting fires.

Dry holes, equipment failures and breakdowns at crucial periods, squabbles and litigation over leases and rights-of-way—these were a few of the myriad problems and setbacks which frequently drained the independent operator's financial resources down to a point well below the danger mark.

In addition, all of us who operated independently often found ourselves facing heavy competition and opposition from major oil firms. Some of these huge companies did not always abide by Marquis of Queensberry rules when they engaged in legal or financial infighting to smother an independent who appeared to be growing too big or too fast.

Wildcatters developed traits and techniques which enabled them to stay in business and to do more than merely hold their own against the petroleum industry's behemoths. We became flexible, adaptable and versatile—adept at improvisation and innovation—if for no other reason than because we *had* to in order to survive. For example, the big companies employed vast numbers of specialists and consultants, administrative personnel and office workers, housing them in large and expensive offices. We, the independents, found our experts among the hardbitten, veteran oil-field workers who formed our prospecting and drilling crews, or we relied on our own judgment and experience to solve our problems as they arose. We did our own administrative and paper work—keeping both to a minimum. As for our offices, these—more often than not—traveled with us in the mud-splotched automobiles we drove from one drilling site to another.

As I have said, I was lucky—very lucky. I made many profitable deals and brought in several producing wells in the months after I first struck oil on the Nancy Taylor Allotment site. The Getty Oil Company prospered. I was named one of the company's directors and elected its secretary, but this did not mean I exchanged my work clothes for a business suit. Notwithstanding my heady new titles, my work was still in the oil fields—and on the drilling rigs. My role in the company's affairs remained the same as it had been. I bought and sold oil leases, and prospected and drilled for oil.

As the Getty Oil Company's wealth increased, so did my own in proportion to my 30-percent share in the firm—and I was also embarked on profitable ventures on my own account. All these things kept me very busy—too busy to pay more than cursory attention to how much money I was actually making. Then, one day, I stopped and took detailed stock of my financial situation. I suddenly realized that I had gone a very long way toward accomplishing what I'd set out to do in September 1914. I had built the foundations of a business of my own in the American oil industry. I was not quite 24, but I had become a successful independent oil operator. And I had made my first million dollars. I was a millionaire!

Until then, my life had been devoted chiefly to growing up, obtaining an education and establishing a business. Now I found I'd made enough money to meet any personal requirements I might conceivably have in the foreseeable future. I made a headstrong snap decision to forget all about work thereafter and to concentrate on playing, on enjoying myself.

My decision was influenced—at least in part—by the fact that there was a war raging in Europe. Although the United States had not yet entered World War One, I felt certain that American participation in the conflict was inevitable. I'd already filed official applications to serve in either the Air Service—my first choice—or the Field Artillery when and if the U.S. declared war. I was sure it would be only a matter of time before I received my orders, and I wanted to relax and have fun before they arrived.

My mother, father and I had made our permanent home in Los Angeles, California, since 1906. I'd attended school and college in California before going on to Oxford and then, later, starting my business career in the Oklahoma oil fields. I loved California and the easy, informal and extremely pleasant life that prevailed there in those days. Thus, it was only natural that I should choose Los Angeles as the place to enjoy the money I'd made in the oil fields.

"I've made my fortune—and I'm going to retire," I announced blandly to my startled parents.

Neither Mother nor Father was pleased with my decision. Both of them had worked very hard in their own youth. When first married, my mother had continued to work as a schoolteacher to help provide my father with the money he needed to put him through law school. Both of them firmly believed that an individual had to work to justify his existence, and that a rich person had to keep his money working to justify its existence. My father tried to impress upon me that a businessman's money is capital to be invested and re-invested.

"You've got to use your money to create, operate and build businesses," he argued. "Your wealth represents potential jobs for countless others—and it can produce wealth and a better life for a great many people as well as for yourself."

I'm afraid I didn't pay much attention to him—then. Later, I was to realize the truth of what he said, but first I had to try things my own way. I owned a spanking new Cadillac road-ster, good clothes and had all the money I could possibly need. I had made up my mind I wanted to play, and with these prerequisites, I encountered no difficulty plunging full tilt into the Southern California–Los Angeles–Hollywood whirl of fun and frolic. Although the United States entered the war, my call-up was first delayed, then postponed by bureaucratic snarls, and finally I was informed that my "services would not be needed." I consequently spent the World War One years playing and enjoying myself.

It took me a while to wake up to the fact that I was only wasting time and that I was bored. By the end of 1918, I was thoroughly fed up. Early in 1919, I was back in the oil busi-ness—not a little abashed by the "I told you so" smile I got from my father when I informed him that, having retired at 24, I was coming out of retirement at 26!

In 1919, oilmen's attention was already shifting from Okla-homa to Southern California, where new producing areas were being discovered and developed. A great new Oil Rush was in the making, and I was among those who wanted to be in on it from the beginning. My initial oil-prospecting venture in Southern California was a fiasco: I drilled my first Cali-fornia well on the Didier Ranch near Puente, but the well proved to be a dry hole.

The luck that had stayed with me in Oklahoma had taken a brief holiday, but it hadn't deserted me. Subsequent tries were considerably more successful. I drilled several wells in the Santa Fe Springs, Torrance, Long Beach and other South-ern California areas, and most of them proved to be pro-ducers, some of them sensational producers.

I spent most of my time in the field working on the drilling rigs with my men, a habit which paid many handsome and unexpected dividends. Not the least of these stemmed from the drilling crews' reactions to the presence of a working boss on the job. The men felt they were partners with the boss in a mutual effort, rather than merely employees of some corporation run by executives they never saw and who had probably never set foot on a drilling platform in their lives. Morale—and production—soared as a result.

This was important, for with new wells being drilled by the hundreds throughout Southern California, there was an acute shortage of experienced oil-field workers. The personnel managers of most large companies engaged in wild scrambles to find the necessary manpower for their operations. They bid frantically against each other in the labor market, offering special inducements and benefits to anyone who'd ever had any experience working on an oil rig. Most oldtimers resented the implication that they had to be bribed with frills to do an honest day's work. They preferred to sign on with wildcatting operators who offered no fancy extras, but who spoke their language and worked side by side with them on the drilling sites.

I'll never forget the time I began drilling on a property not far from the site on which a major oil company was drilling a well. Carrying its employee inducement program to ludicrous extremes, the firm had designed and built what its press agents glowingly described as the last word in drilling rigs. The entire rig was steamheated all the way up to the crown block. A neatly raked gravel drive led to the site. There were hot showers for the men and even a laundry that washed their work clothes while they waited!

Early one afternoon, not long after I'd spudded my well, a grizzled roughneck appeared on my site and announced that he wanted to see the boss. When I was pointed out to him, he came over and wasted no words asking me for a job.

"Are you working now?" I asked.

"Yeah," came the sour reply.

"Where?"

"Over there," the roughneck replied, nodding his head toward the deluxe drilling rig. There were no home comforts available for my crew, and I told the man so. And, I added, I couldn't understand why he would want to leave a job that offered such luxuries for one on my relatively primitive operation.

"I've been on that rig for four months," the roughneck growled unhappily. "And we've only gotten down four thousand feet!" I laughed. Four thousand feet in four months was a ridiculously slow rate for drilling through the type of soil formations to be found in that particular field.

"How long do you think it'll take me to get down that far?" I asked.

"From the looks of you—about ten days!" the oldtimer answered with a broad grin. "That's why I'd rather work for you than for that cream-puff outfit over there . . .!"

He got the job, and stayed on my payroll for many years. As a footnote to the story, I might add that my well was drilled in record time and proved a good producer. The "last word" in drilling rigs brought in a dry hole and was finally abandoned.

Another good example of what close teamwork and mutual confidence between boss and crew could accomplish can be found in the story of how my men and I licked the "insoluble" problem of a certain oil lease.

The lease was on a tiny piece of property in the midst of a forest of oil wells in the rich Seal Beach, California, field. By some fluke, the lease had been overlooked by the firms which were operating there. A company in which I held a substantial interest acquired the lease, but was about to write it off as a dead loss. Everyone agreed that nothing could ever be done with the property. In the first place, it was a plot barely larger than the floor area of a small house. In the second, the only right-of-way providing access to a road was over a strip of ground several hundred feet long but less than four feet wide. It was impossible to get supplies and equipment to the property by truck over this constricted path. Even if it had been possible, the postage-stamp-sized plot would not have accommodated a regular-sized derrick and drilling rig. The companies holding leases on adjacent properties refused to grant any right-of-way over their sites, for if a producing well was brought in, it might diminish the production of their own wells, since it would be pumping oil from the same pool.

"Forget the lease," associates with whom I discussed the

matter advised me. "You'll never get a well drilled there—not in a million years."

Stubbornly, I insisted there must be a way; I put the problem before the men in whom I had the greatest confidence, the members of one of my drilling crews. They listened to me, and their reaction was the same as mine. They considered the problem an irresistible challenge.

"Let's go up and look at things, boss," a hardbitten driller grunted. "We'll find some way—don't worry." Several men and I went to survey the situation firsthand, and we found that it did look fairly hopeless.

"I guess we could drill the well with an undersized rig," the driller mused after thinking things over. "If you could get somebody to design and build it, we could set it up—but I can't figure how we're going to bring everything we need in from the road . . ."

The obstacle provided by the limited right-of-way seemed insuperable, until my mind began to turn over the driller's suggestion about a miniature drilling rig. If we could drill with a miniature rig, then why couldn't we solve our transportation problem with a miniature railway? It was a perfect solution: A narrow-gauge track and a car or two on which to bring the disassembled "baby" derrick and supplies and equipment from the road to the drilling site.

Mulish obstinacy? A desire to prove that we were able to accomplish what everyone else considered impossible? Possibly—even probably. But both the miniature rig and the miniature railway were procured. The former was moved in sections over the latter and assembled by hand on the microscopic plot of ground. The well was drilled—and a fair profit was eventually realized on the unusual operation.

I recall other memorable strikes during the 1920s. Among them is the one I made in the so-called Athens Field in the southern suburbs of Los Angeles. I acquired the plot in question for something over $12,000. Because I was operating entirely on my own account and knew that I would be stretching my available cash resources thin before completing the first well, I elected to act as my own drilling superintendent. Among the men I hired for my crew were three of the finest drillers in the oil industry: Walter Phillips, Oscar Prowell and "Spot" McMurdo. We completed the first well on February 16, 1925, at a depth of 4350 feet for an initial daily yield of 1500 barrels. A short while later, I brought in the second well on the site for an initial production of 2000 barrels per day. In the next nine years, the two wells on the Athens property were to show over $400,000 excess recovery—clear profit over and above all costs and expenses.

Even more spectacular is the story of the Cleaver Lease in Alamitos Heights, which I bought with a personal check for $8000 in October 1926 from a man who had purchased it for $4000 only a few days before and who wanted to make a quick profit.

I spudded Well Number One on February 21, 1927, and subsequently drilled three more wells on the property. All proved exceptional producers, bringing up a total of more than 17,000 barrels daily. Between 1927 and 1939, excess recovery on the Cleaver Lease wells was nearly $800,000— a 10,000-percent profit on my original investment. Yet, within a few weeks after the first well came in, I was not only close to losing a fortune, but also close to losing the lease itself. Behind this apparent paradox lie two stories. One illustrates what the average wildcatter faced when he jousted with certain major oil companies. The other proves that while some large firms had no compunctions about strangling an independent operator, others were ready and willing to give him a break—and even a helping hand.

As soon as I'd brought in Cleaver Well Number One— which produced an impressive 5100 barrels a day—I cast about to find a buyer for my crude production. To my dismay, the firms I approached refused to deal with me. The motives behind this evident boycott became infuriatingly clear within a few days, when I received several calls from brokers offering to buy the Cleaver Lease at a very low price. The brokers refused to name the principals they represented.

By then, I was an old hand in the petroleum industry. I recognized all the classic signs indicating a well-organized squeeze play. Certain interests wanted my lease. Either I sold out at a ridiculously low price, or I would be left without any market for the oil produced by the wells on the property.

Unable to sell my oil, I had to find some way to store it. The only storage facilities available in the Los Angeles area were in a defunct refinery—two storage tanks with a total 155,000-barrel capacity, which I immediately leased. In the meantime, even while I was vainly seeking a buyer for the 5100 barrels of crude my Well Number One was producing every 24 hours, Well Number Two came in for a 5000-barrel daily production. This was followed in short order by Number Three, which produced 5100 barrels a day, then by Number Four, the runt of the litter, which brought up 2100 barrels daily. This production rate was rapidly filling the two storage tanks—and I was still unable to find an outlet for the oil. I knew that when the tanks were topped off, I'd have no choice but to shut down my operation entirely.

Obviously, I was receiving no income from the four wells. My fluid cash resources—already strained by drilling costs—dwindled rapidly as I paid for leasing the tanks and for trucking my crude several miles from wells to storage. The situation could have easily turned into financial disaster. I decided to make a frontal attack on one of the biggest of all the major oil companies—Shell Oil. By a fortunate coincidence, Sir George Legh-Jones, then the Shell Company's president, happened to be visiting in Los Angeles. In desperation, I aimed high, asked for an interview with him personally, and was informed that he would be happy to see me during his visit.

A warm, friendly man, Sir George listened attentively to what I had to say. The deepening scowl that etched across his face as he heard me was all the proof I needed that his firm was not a party to the boycott and that he heartily disapproved of such tactics. When I finished talking, he smiled his reassurance.

"Relax," he grinned. "We'll help you."

As a starter, the company would buy the next 1,750,000 barrels of crude oil produced by my Cleaver Lease wells, Sir George told me. In addition, a pipeline would be constructed to link my wells with the Shell Oil Company's pipeline network—and construction work was to commence the very next day.

Sir George and the Shell Company were as good as their word. Shell's work crews arrived on my Cleaver site bright and early the following morning and started to lay the pipeline. The boycott was broken—and the Cleaver Lease was safely and profitably mine!

As the 1920s drew to a close, the American petroleum industry began to undergo a radical change. It was rapidly growing more complex; the costs of finding and producing oil were spiraling ever higher. Much greater capital expenditures were needed to purchase leases, machinery and equipment and to finance exploration and drilling. Most oil pools that lay near the surface in known oil belts had been located and were being exploited. It was necessary to prospect ever farther afield and to drill ever deeper to find oil.

There were many mergers and consolidations of oil companies. Some independent operators were falling by the wayside. Others were selling out to big oil companies. There was also a strange, ominous undercurrent running through the entire U.S. economy. The stock market listed shares at fantastic highs, but there were warnings and forebodings of economic trouble ahead.

It was a critical period for all wildcatters and a particularly difficult one for me. I had to look after my own mushrooming business interests—my own leases, producing wells and companies. Then, through the years, I'd bought sizable blocks of stock in my father's companies as well. Now, his health began to fail, and I found it increasingly necessary to take an active part in managing the operations of these companies.

In 1929, the stock market crashed. The following year, my father suffered a stroke. Although he was over 75, he fought death bravely and grimly for several weeks, but the battle was lost on May 31, 1930, when he passed away. My mother and I were allowed but little time to grieve. We had to keep his business going and his companies operating. The Federal Government pressed for rapid settlement of the inheritance taxes on the estate. These and many other matters demanded immediate attention and all were complicated by the economic factor of the deepening Depression. Many advised me to liquidate everything—to sell out not only my late father's holdings, but my own firms and interests as well.

"The business situation can only get worse," they predicted. "The economy is going to disintegrate completely!"

I didn't see things that way at all. I was convinced the nation's economy was essentially sound—that though it might sag lower in the near future, it would eventually bounce

back, healthier than ever. I thought it was the time to buy—
not sell.

Many oil stocks were selling at all-time lows; they were
spectacular bargains. I began to envision the organization of
a completely integrated and self-contained oil business, one
embracing not only exploration and production—the operations in which I'd been exclusively engaged until that time—
but also transportation, refining and even retail marketing.

In business, as in politics, it is never easy to go against the
beliefs and attitudes held by the majority. The businessman
who moves counter to the tide of prevailing opinion must
expect to be obstructed, derided and damned. So it was with
me when, in the depths of the U.S. economic slump of the
1930s, I resolved to make large-scale stock purchases and
build a self-contained oil business. My friends and acquaintances—to say nothing of my competitors—felt my buying
spree would prove a fatal mistake. Then, when I announced
my intention to buy into one of the seven major oil companies
operating in California, even those who had been my supporters in the past were inclined to believe I had taken leave
of my senses.

Major oil companies could, and often did, buy out independent operators' firms. But for an independent operator to
buy a major oil company? That was heresy—an attempt to
turn the established order upside down!

Nonetheless, I went ahead with my plans, for I was looking
to the future. The oil companies I controlled or in which I
held substantial interests were engaged exclusively in finding
oil and getting it out of the ground. To insure markets for
this oil and for that to be produced by new wells drilled in
the future, it seemed a wise move to invest in a company
which needed crude oil and which also had adequate refining
and marketing facilities. There were only seven such companies in California—all majors.

The list was headed by the Standard Oil Company of
California—obviously far too big a chunk for any independent
to bite off and digest. The same held true for the Shell Oil
Company. The next possibility was the Union Oil Company,
but this firm had its own crude-oil sources. So did the General
Petroleum Company which, in any event, was virtually a
closed corporation, and its stock was not available for pur-

chase. That left three firms: Richfield Oil—then in receivership and consequently not a very tempting prospect; the Texas Oil Company, which was amply supplied with its own crude; and, lastly, the Tide Water Associated Oil Company.

Tide Water Associated seemed the logical choice. The company met only half its refineries' crude requirements from its own reserves, buying the rest from other producers. Tide Water also had a good marketing organization and its products enjoyed a good reputation with the consuming public.

I saw great advantages in linking up with Tide Water— advantages which would be shared by all concerned, and most particularly Tide Water's 34,668 individual shareholders and the consumers who bought the company's products.

I began my Tide Water campaign in March 1932, by purchasing 1200 common shares at $2.50 per share. Within the next six weeks, I'd increased my holdings to 41,000 shares. Nearly 20 years were to pass before I gained clear-cut control of the firm. In that time, my producing companies and I would buy millions of shares of Tide Water common. I didn't guess wrong when I started buying at depressed 1932 prices. In the next five years, Tide Water's common shares rose to more than $16—and eventually each share came to be worth many times that amount.

It was not easy to gain control of the Tide Water Associated Oil Company. Many risks were taken, much opposition encountered, many no-holds-barred proxy and legal battles were fought. Countless critical situations developed. The outcome was often in doubt.

My first attempt to obtain a voice in Tide Water's management was made in May 1932. I went to the annual stockholders' meeting armed with my own 41,000 shares, plus a proxy for 126,000 additional shares. At the last moment, the proxy was revoked. My efforts ended in failure. I bought more stock and tried to sell my ideas to Tide Water's directors. They, however, did not see things my way and dug in for a long, hard fight. Why? Well, I suppose there were several reasons. First of all, I was an outsider. I'd had little or no experience in the heady atmosphere of board rooms.

"Paul Getty should stay where he belongs—on a drilling rig" a Tide Water director supposedly snorted when told I was buying the company's stock right and left. I fear there were others on the board even less kindly disposed toward me and my ambitions.

I'd studied Tide Water's organization and operations carefully and recommended that the company make certain changes and practice certain economies. These recommendations, apparently too radical to suit the conservative directors, caused considerable resentment.

I'd also concluded that much of Tide Water's refining plant was obsolescent and would soon be obsolete. I believed the company should make provisions for modernization and replacement, but management was reluctant to make capital expenditures during the business slump. The directors called it "necessary caution." I viewed it as short-sighted and dangerous penny-pinching.

By 1933, Getty interests owned nearly 260,000 Tide Water shares—a block too large to be ignored. I was elected to the company's board, but it was a hollow victory. I was only one among many, and the other directors were still ranged solidly against me and my proposals. I continued to buy Tide Water stock. Proxy fights, lawsuits and countersuits ensued. Injunctions, restraining orders and writs flew in blizzards.

By late 1937, Getty interests owned enough stock to obtain a voice in management. Three years later, we held 1,734,577 shares—a shade over one fourth the voting stock, and many changes I proposed were being implemented. By 1951, I held enough Tidewater stock to have numerical control. (By then, the "Associated" had been dropped from the company name and "Tide Water" contracted into a single word.) Two years later, with all but one director elected by Getty interests, the campaign was finally over. Today, Tidewater's assets exceed $800,000,000.

In 1938, I turned momentarily from the oil business and bought the Hotel Pierre in New York City, purchasing it for $2,350,000, less than one fourth its original (1929–1930) cost. Later, I bought several hundred acres of land in Acapulco, Mexico, where I eventually built the Pierre Marques Hotel on Revolcadero Beach. These, contrary to reports which have me owning a string of hotels, are the only ones I own.

In 1937, as part of the Tide Water campaign, I obtained control of a firm known as the Mission Corporation. Among Mission's holdings was a 57-percent interest in the Skelly Oil

Company, a major oil firm with headquarters in Tulsa, Oklahoma. Thus, almost as a windfall, I acquired the controlling interest in a company with a 1937 net income of $6,400,000—and which, today, has more than $330,000,000 in assets.

But this is not the whole story. Among Skelly Oil's subsidiaries was the Spartan Aircraft Corporation, a Tulsa concern engaged since 1928 in manufacturing aircraft and training pilots and navigators. I paid my first visit to the Spartan plant on December 7, 1939. Its aircraft-manufacturing operations were rather limited; there were only some 60 workers employed in the factory. The pilot training school was much more active. It was, in fact, the largest private flying school in the U.S.

I'd just returned from a trip to Europe, which was already at war. I was convinced that the United States would eventually have to throw its weight into the war against the Axis. Consequently, I felt Spartan Aircraft would have an increasingly important role in the nation's defense program—but I could not guess then how very important it was destined to be.

Two years to the day after my first visit to Spartan, the Japanese attacked Pearl Harbor and the United States was at war. It was in that same month that my beloved mother died. It was a heavy blow. Although I was by then almost 50, I felt the loss as keenly as though I had still been a youngster.

War news filled the newspapers. I had not been allowed to serve in World War One, and I now hoped for the chance to serve in the second world conflict. I had studied celestial navigation and had owned—at various times in my life—three yachts, the largest a 260-foot, 1500-tonner with a crew of 45. On the basis of this, I volunteered for service in the United States Navy. To my chagrin, I was politely but firmly informed that the Navy didn't have much use for a middle-aged businessman unless he was willing to take a routine, shore-based administrative job. After exhausting all other avenues, I obtained an interview with Navy Secretary Frank Knox and pleaded my case. I told him I wanted a Navy commission and sea duty.

"You qualify for a commission as an administrative or supply officer," Secretary Knox declared. "But sea duty is out of the question." He paused and studied me closely. "I understand you hold a large interest in the Spartan Aircraft Corporation," he said after a moment. I agreed that I did.

"The Armed Forces must have every aircraft factory in large-scale production as soon as possible," he told me. "The most important service you can render the war effort is to drop all your other business interests and take over direct personal management of Spartan."

I arrived in Tulsa as the working president of Spartan in February 1942. There was a tremendous amount to be done and very little time in which to do it. Manufacturing facilities—including factory space—had to be expanded, machinery and tools obtained, engineers and technicians recruited and workers hired and trained by the thousands. Despite bottlenecks, shortages and setbacks, peak production was attained in less than 18 months.

I remained in active and direct charge of Spartan's operations throughout the War. Before it ended, the Spartan flying school was training as many as 1700 fledgling aviators at a time. By V-J Day, the Spartan factory—employing more than 5500 workers at the peak—had turned out a vast array of airplane parts and components on subcontracts from major aircraft firms. Among these were: 5800 sets of elevators, ailerons and rudders for B-24 bombers; 2500 engine-mount sets for P-47 fighters; Curtiss dive-bomber cowlings by the hundreds; Douglas dive-bomber control surfaces by the thousands; wings for Grumman Wildcat fighters; tail booms for Lockheed P-38 pursuits. Spartan also produced N-1 primary trainers on prime contract.

Spartan's production record brought high commendations from the Armed Forces—tributes to the efficiency and loyalty of the men and women who'd worked for the firm and who did their part in helping to win the War. I stayed on at Spartan until 1948 to nurse the firm through the pangs of reconversion to peacetime production of house trailers. Then once more I went back to my first and greatest business love—oil.

My oil companies were prospering and were larger and more active than ever before, but it was time for additional expansion. Vast demands had been made on America's oil reserves by the War, and post-War petroleum consumption was rising sharply throughout the world. Oil prospectors were fanning out—to Canada, Central and South America, Africa and the Middle East—searching for new oil sources. Instinct, hunch, luck—call it what you will—told me the Middle East was the most promising locale, the best bet, for oil exploration. I had almost obtained an oil concession in the Middle East in the 1930s, but had allowed my chance to go by. Now I decided to seek a concession to prospect and drill there and make up for the opportunity I had lost. In February 1949, Getty interests obtained a 60-year concession on a half interest in the so-called Neutral Zone, an arid, virtually uninhabited and barely explored desert region lying between Saudi Arabia and Kuwait on the Persian Gulf.

The concession was granted by His Majesty, Ibn Saud, king of Saudi Arabia. In immediate consideration for the right to explore and drill for oil in the Neutral Zone, the Saudi Arabian Government received $12,500,000. It was a gargantuan risk and many people in the petroleum industry once again openly predicted I would bankrupt my firms and myself.

Four years and $18,000,000 were needed before we brought in our first producing well in the Neutral Zone. But, by 1954, I could relax and enjoy a private last laugh at the expense of those who had prophesied my ruin. The Neutral Zone has proved to be one of the world's most valuable oil properties. Well after well has come in and petroleum geologists conservatively estimate proven reserves in place in the region covered by my concession to exceed 13 billion barrels!

With this tremendous reserve and with producing wells in the Middle East and elsewhere bringing up millions of barrels of crude oil annually, it has been necessary to expand even further in other directions. The companies have had to build and buy additional refineries to handle the enormous crude-oil production. Pipelines, storage facilities, housing projects for workers and innumerable other installations and facilities have been built or are abuilding.

A $200,000,000 Tidewater Oil Company refinery was completed at Wilmington, Delaware, in 1957. Another Tidewater refinery near San Francisco has been modernized at a cost of $60,000,000. There is a new 40,000-barrel-a-day refinery in

Gaeta, Italy, and another with a 20,000-barrel-a-day capacity in Denmark.

In 1954 and 1955, construction began on the first vessels in a fleet of supertankers. Several of these have been completed and are now in operation. This tanker-construction program is proceeding apace. Tonnage afloat and now under construction exceeds 1,000,000 deadweight tons. Among the ships are truly giant supertankers displacing upwards of 70,000 tons.

The Getty interests have recently built spanking new office buildings in Los Angeles, California; Tulsa, Oklahoma; and New York City—at a cost approaching $40,000,000. Regardless of what they produce, plants and businesses owned by Getty interests are orientated to steady expansion. Management is constantly seeking ways and means to increase output, and large-scale projects are under way to develop new products and to find new applications and uses for old ones. By no means the least of the activities in which the companies are engaged are oil and mineral explorations, which are being conducted energetically on four continents.

This, then, is the story of how I chose my road to success and how I traveled it from my wildcatting days in the Oklahoma oil fields, of how I've built my business and made my fortune. To it, I would like to add a brief, highly personal—and mildly rueful—footnote.

For years I had managed—at least on the whole—to avoid personal publicity. Or rather, since I did nothing either to seek or evade it, I suppose it would be more accurate to say that personal publicity avoided me. This state of peaceful near-anonymity ended suddenly and forever in October 1957, when *Fortune* magazine published an article listing the wealthiest people in the United States. My name headed the list, and the article labeled me a billionaire and "The Richest Man in America." Subsequently, other publications gave me the even more grandiloquent title of "The Richest Man in the World."

Since then, I've been besieged by requests to reveal exactly how much money I have. I'm seldom believed when I reply in all honesty that I don't know, that there is no way I *can* know. Most of my wealth is invested in the businesses I own or control; I make no claims about the extent of my wealth and I really don't care how rich I am.

Today, the companies are thriving, and they're carrying out ambitious programs for further expansion. My primary concern and main interest lie in making certain that these companies continue to grow so that they can provide more employment and produce more goods and services for the benefit of all. My associates and I are convinced that the over-all economic trend is up and that despite the alarums and fears plaguing our era, the world is on the threshold of a prosperity greater than any in its history.

YOU
CAN MAKE
A MILLION TODAY

The door to the American Millionaire's Club is not locked. Contrary to popular modern belief, it is still quite possible for the successful individual to make his million—and more. There will always be room for the man with energy and imagination, the man who can successfully implement new ideas into new products and services.

Anyone who has achieved success is frequently asked the same question by the people he meets: "How can I—or others—do it, too?"

When I tell them how I began building the foundations of my own business as a wildcatting operator more than four decades ago, they usually reply:

"But you were lucky—you started in business at a time when it was still possible to make millions. You couldn't do it nowadays. No one could."

I never cease to be astounded by the prevalence of this negative—and, in my opinion, totally erroneous—attitude among supposedly intelligent people. Certainly, there is a tremendous mass of evidence to prove that imaginative, resourceful and dynamic young men have more opportunities to achieve wealth and success in businsss today than ever before in our history. Countless alert and aggressive businessmen have proved this by making their fortunes in a wide variety of business endeavors in recent years.

One man I know was a lower-bracket corporation executive when, in 1953, he heard of the development of a new, particularly tough and versatile plastic. He perceived that it would make an excellent and economical substitute for certain costly building materials. Using his savings and some borrowed money to buy the manufacturing license and to provide the necessary initial working capital, he went into business for himself producing and distributing the plastic. By 1960, he was personally worth well over a million dollars.

John S. Larkins, a young engineer, took over the Elox Corporation—a tiny Royal Oak, Michigan, electronics-equipment manufacturing firm—in 1951. Seeing that there was a great and constantly growing need for electronic-control devices in industry, Larkins concentrated on developing and producing these items. Within six years, he had increased his company's gross sales from $194,000 to more than $2,200,000 per year.

In 1942, Charles Bluhdorn, then 16, began his career as a $15-a-week cotton-brokerage clerk. By 1950, he had made his first million on his own—mostly by importing coffee from Brazil. Today, he is the kingpin of multitentacled Gulf & Western Industries, whose annual sales well exceed a billion dollars.

There are innumerable such modern-day success stories. Among those with which I am personally acquainted, none is more telling or to the point than that of the late Melville (Jack) Forrester.

Jack Forrester served with distinction as an OSS agent in Europe during World War Two. After V-J Day, he found himself in Paris, out of work and low on funds. He finally obtained a job as a sort of bird-dogging contact man with a large investment firm, the World Commerce Corporation. Forrester toured Europe, the Middle East and Asia, looking for promising projects and enterprises in which World Commerce Corporation could invest money. A shrewd and astute businessman, he did so well that within a few years he was made president of the firm's French subsidiary, World Commerce Corporation of France. I had known Jack before the War. I met him again in Paris in 1949. He told me what he had been doing since V-J Day.

"How would you like to do some work for me?" I asked him.

"I don't know much about the oil business," he replied with a grin. "But I suppose I can learn fast enough."

Jack did learn fast—and well. After 1949, he conducted many delicate and important negotiations for several of my companies. He was instrumental in obtaining valuable oil concessions and prepared and smoothed the way for many other operations and transactions including deals for tanker, refinery and pipeline construction.

In 1945, Jack Forrester was an ex-OSS man without a job and with very little money. He was just another of the many millions of men who were trying to "reconvert" to peacetime existence. At his untimely death in 1964, he had become an eminently successful businessman—and a millionaire.

There are examples galore to prove that it can be done, that success in business and even "making a million"—or millions—are entirely realizable goals for young men starting out today. I consider myself neither prophet nor pundit, economist nor political scientist. I speak simply as a practical, working businessman. The careful, continuing study and evaluation of American and international business conditions and trends are, however, among my most important duties and responsibilities to the companies I control. Basing my opinion on the information I have been able to gather throughout the years, I believe that, barring the cataclysmic unforeseen, the outlook for business is good and that it will become even better as time goes on. I feel that farsighted, progressive—and, above all, open-minded—American businessmen, be they beginners or veterans, have ample reason to be optimistic about their prospects and profits for years and even decades to come. I say this fully aware that, in some American business circles, it has long been fashionable—if not downright mandatory—to bemoan lack of opportunity and the stifling of free-enterprise capitalism.

"Confiscatory taxation," "excessive labor costs," "unfair foreign competition" and "creeping socialism" are the "causes" most often cited for what the doom-mongers would have us believe is the imminent disintegration of the American Free Enterprise System. To my way of thinking, all this is sheer nonsense. The complaints are merely convenient alibis for the unimaginative, the incompetent, the near-sighted and narrow-minded and the lazy. True, taxes are too high—and far too numerous. One of these days—and soon—our entire tax system will have to be overhauled from top to bottom. A logical, equitable tax program will have to be devised to replace the insane hodgepodge of Federal, state, county and city levies that make life a fiscal nightmare for everyone. In the meantime, however, businessmen will just have to live with the situation. Let's be honest about it: that they *can* live with it is obvious enough. Income taxes—the most abused whipping boys—are, after all, levied only on profits. There are proportionately more well-to-do businessmen in the United States than ever before. I've never heard of a single American firm that had to close its doors because of taxation alone.

Labor costs are also high, but I've often observed that the man who complains the loudest about excessive wages is the same one who spends fortunes on advertising and sales campaigns to sell his products to the millions. How on earth he expects the workers who form the bulk of those millions to buy his chinaware, garden furniture or whirling-spray pipe-cleaners unless they are well paid is beyond my comprehension. Labor is entitled to good pay, to its share of the wealth it helps produce. Unless there is a prosperous "working class," there can be no mass-markets and no mass-sales for merchants or manufacturers—and there will be precious little prosperity for anyone. For its part, labor must understand that high wages are justified—and can remain high—only if workers maintain high levels and standards of production. And, as long as we're talking about things that are high, I might add that I, for one, think it's high time both capital and labor realized these basic home truths and ceased their eternal and costly wrangling. Whether either likes it or not, one cannot exist in its present form without the other. I doubt very seriously if either would find the totalitarian alternatives to the existing system very pleasant or palatable.

As for foreign competition, it has long been my experience that competition of any kind is promptly labeled unfair when it begins to hurt those businessmen who do not possess the imagination and energy to meet it. Competition—foreign or otherwise—exists to be met and bested. Competition—the stiffer and more vigorous the better—is the stimulus, the very basis, of the free-enterprise system. Without competition, business would stagnate.

These facts are conveniently ignored by those individuals and pressure groups who loudly demand that the Federal Government do something about "unfair" foreign competition. The "something" they want the Government to "do" is, of course, to raise sky-high tariff walls which would prevent foreign countries from trading with us—about as nearsighted a policy as one could imagine.

Creeping socialism? That particular plaint is proven to be false and without foundation by the very fact that there are so many more free-enterprise-system American businessmen to voice it today than there were ten, twenty or more years ago.

In short, I can't see any validity in the arguments advanced by the pessimists and defeatists. But then, calamity howlers have always been with us, chanting one dismal and discouraging chorus or another.

When I purchased the Hotel Pierre, located on Manhattan's swank Fifth Avenue at 61st Street for $2,350,000, it was New York's most modern hotel. No crystal ball was needed to show that this was an excellent buy. The country was rapidly emerging from the Depression; business conditions were improving steadily. Business and personal travel were bound to increase greatly. There had been very little hotel construction in New York for several years, and none was planned for the immediate future. The Pierre was a bargain—and a hotel with a great potential. But the gloom-and-doom chaps were too busy titillating their masochistic streaks with pessimistic predictions of worse times to come to recognize such bargains as this when they saw them.

I began negotiations for the purchase of the Hotel Pierre in October 1938 and took possession the following May. At today's land and construction costs, between 25 and 35 million dollars would be needed to duplicate the Pierre in New York City.

I'm not crowing; I'm merely trying to show that there are always opportunities through which businessmen can profit handsomely if they will only recognize and seize them—and if they will disregard the pessimistic auguries of self-appointed prophets of doom.

Conditions are much different now than they were in 1938, 1932 or 1915. Just the same, the last things that American business needs are complaints, alibis and defeatist philosophies.

What American business *does* need—and in ever-increasing numbers—are young businessmen who are willing and able to assume the responsibilities of progressive, vigorous industrial and commercial leadership. The rewards awaiting such men are practically limitless. There is plenty of room at the top. That figurative Millionaire's Club has an unlimited number of vacancies on its membership rolls. That these aren't being filled faster is, I'm afraid, due largely to the fact that too many potentially highly qualified young applicants give up before they start. They listen to cautionary defeatism instead of opening their eyes to the opportunities around them. They are apparently blind to the many examples provided by those who have made and are making their fortunes.

As I've said, I started my own business career in the petroleum industry as a wildcatter, and oil has remained my main business interest. I find it discomfiting that so many young men today have an idea that the era of the relatively small-time wildcatter is over. Actually, nothing could be further from the truth.

Oil is a funny thing. It is likely to turn up in the most unlikely places. There are many areas in the United States where an enterprising wildcatter is quite likely to find oil—and to strike it rich. Admittedly, most structures in recognized oil belts have been located and are being exploited. On the other hand, there are many localities which have received little or no serious attention from oil prospectors.

At the time I started wildcatting, "everyone" said there was no oil in the Oklahoma Red Beds. By the same token, 30 or 40 years ago, oil operators got it into their heads that there was no oil in Oregon, Washington, Idaho, Iowa or Utah—to name only some states—and passed them up. This belief has influenced oil exploration ever since. That it's a theory without much fact to support it is proven by the fact that only a few years back, oil prospectors finally began drilling test wells in Utah—and discovered oil.

There are many opportunities for the knowledgeable small-scale wildcatter today. While the oil prospector has to do his exploration outside recognized—and thus already exploited—oil belts, scientific and technological advances have made the business of looking and drilling for oil easier than it was years ago. Petroleum geology, an infant and at best uncertain science in 1914, has made fantastic strides. The modern geologist has the knowledge, experience and equipment that make it possible for him to spot the presence of oil with a much-better-than-fair degree of accuracy. It's true that most of the oil that lay close to the surface has been located, and that wells have to be drilled to much greater depths than was necessary in the early part of the Twentieth Century. On the other hand, using modern drilling rigs and equipment, an oil operator can drill to 6,000 feet more quickly and more cheaply than I drilled to 2,500 feet in 1916—and in those days, a dollar was worth far more than it is now.

But the oil industry is by no means the only business that offers golden opportunities to the beginner today. All the potentials for an era of unprecedented business activity and prosperity are present—for those who are open-minded and imaginative enough to recognize them. Rapidly expanding populations at home and abroad and the awakening desires of human beings all over the world to better their living conditions and to raise their living standards are guarantees that there will be ever-expanding markets for goods and services of every kind for many years to come. The gigantic strides being made almost daily by science and technology provide the means whereby those goods and services may be produced and distributed more cheaply, in better quality and in greater quantity.

There are still fantastic demands to be met at home. No one can rightfully say that American business has discharged its responsibilities and done its job until every employable citizen has steady, full-time employment and until every American family is well-fed, well-clothed, well-housed and able to live in comfort and without fear. I do not hesitate to predict that many young men who read this will make their fortunes and spend their entire business careers dealing exclusively with domestic markets, meeting domestic demands. On the other hand, I am of the opinion that the brightest horizons of American business are to be found outside the United States, in international trade.

Newspapers all over the world have given a great deal of prominence to stories about increasing unemployment and recession in the U.S. and the "dollar-drain" caused by an unfavorable United States–foreign trade balance. Many remedies are being suggested to correct these situations. Among them are demands for "emergency" measures designed to cut down or even halt imports of many materials and products from foreign lands.

"The United States must cut all its foreign imports to an absolute minimum," a junketing American businessman declared to me not long ago. "That's the only way American business will be able to survive."

I'm afraid he was very surprised when I told him that, in my opinion, the policy he advocated was tantamount to economic suicide. The way I see it, the long-term solution to our country's economic problems lies in *more*, not less, foreign trade. For the long haul, U.S. business will have to embark on a gigantic, farsighted program of international trade, seeking and expanding markets in foreign lands. There is no room for isolationist business philosophies in our present era. The world has grown far too small. The American economy cannot batten upon itself; American business must develop new and more overseas trade. And, in order to sell to other countries, we must also buy from them. It's that simple. I firmly believe that the young businessman who can rid his mind of outdated, preconceived notions and gear his thinking to these needs of the times will reap tremendous rewards. He will make his millions. For, despite rumors and reports to the contrary, most foreign countries want very much to have us sell them goods. They *want* to buy from us.

I travel extensively abroad, and I have business interests on five continents. I have found very little evidence to indicate there is any lessening of demand for products which bear the "Made in U.S.A." label. The American way of life remains the golden symbol of good living everywhere. To duplicate or imitate it is still the goal of most people in foreign lands—and the promise that they will do so is still the most glowingly attractive and effective promise foreign government leaders and politicians can make to their own people. Even Russians admit this when they make predictions that Soviet production and living standards will equal or surpass prevailing American levels. Whatever may have happened to American political prestige in recent years, there has been no appreciable loss of what, for want of a better term, I would call American "product prestige."

The proofs of all this are plain enough to anyone who lives or travels abroad with open eyes and an open mind.

Most of the world outside the Iron Curtain happily sips American cola and hopes some day to own a Sheaffer pen. American automobiles are still status symbols for those who own them in foreign countries—and so are American refrigerators, washing machines, TV sets and a host of other items. Arrow shirts, Colgate toothpaste, Gillette razors and blades—these and a thousand and one other American trademarked products are high on the preferred lists of foreign shoppers. In Communist countries, even such commonplace American-made items as ballpoint pens, lipsticks and nylon stockings fetch black-market prices ten or more times their open-market cost. Any American who has resided abroad for any length of time knows what it is to be bombarded by requests that he order this or that item from the States.

The demand is there—have no doubt about that. Foreign markets are wide open to the enterprising American businessman—more so now than ever before because the wealth and buying power of people in many foreign lands have multiplied many times in the last decade.

"But we can't compete with foreign manufacturers," a U.S. industrialist complained to me recently. "They can always undersell us."

First of all, it's not true that foreign manufacturers can "always" undersell American producers. Take just two random examples. American coal, mined by highly paid American miners, is sold in a great many parts of Europe at a lower price than English coal, which is produced by English miners who earn far less than their U.S. counterparts. An Italian-made shirt of a quality equal to that of a five-dollar American shirt sells for more than eight dollars in Italy.

The secret of competing in the foreign market lies in realizing that no foreign country has yet truly mastered the techniques of high-quality mass-production to the degree that we have. Nor do many foreign businessmen understand the theory behind volume turnover at comparatively small per-sale profits. In the main, they still cling to the long-outmoded principle of making large profits per sale and contenting themselves with relatively small turnover.

Unquestionably, import duties levied by many foreign countries often raise the prices on American goods well above those of like items produced within the countries themselves.

As I see it, enterprising American businessmen can best serve their own—and the public's—interest by demanding that the U.S. Government use all the resources at its disposal to prevail upon other countries to lower or abolish their import duties on American products. This—not the raising of our own tariff walls—will provide a bulwark against recession and unemployment.

At the same time, it is the American businessman's job to devise new means and techniques which will enable him to produce more at lower cost while rigorously maintaining traditional American standards of quality. Then, he must sell his product abroad just as imaginatively and energetically as he does at home.

"But how is it possible to reduce production costs when wages and prices on everything from raw materials to machinery are constantly rising?" is a question I've heard more times than I'd care to count. I maintain that production can always be increased and costs can always be cut if one knows enough about his business to know where to look for waste and inefficiency. There are always means whereby economies may be achieved without lowering standards of quality.

To start with, it's an old manufacturing law that when production is doubled, production costs are automatically reduced by 20 percent. I hardly think any further comment is needed on this. Then, there is administrative overhead—a cost item which can almost invariably stand a great deal of judicious pruning. It's very seldom necessary for an assistant vice-president's secretary to have her own secretary. I've run my business personally for decades—and I've never found any need for more than one secretary. Truth to tell, much that is dictated and then typed in multiple copies could be passed on faster, more efficiently and more cheaply by the simple expedient of dialing a telephone. And I'll wager that most firms could slash their "entertainment" budgets by 50 percent or more without losing a single sale. I can take a drink or two myself, but I've observed that one generally does far more business in 15 minutes over a cup of coffee than he can possibly do in three hours over a six-martini lunch.

There is no Federal statute that requires all salesmen and executives in a company to fly "deluxe" wherever they go, when they can get where they're going just as fast, almost as comfortably—and at an impressively lower cost—on tourist flights. There are many other areas in which the smart young businessman will find that he can effect important economies. There is always room for improvement—and for savings—in business, be it in the home office, the plant or wherever.

I'm not advocating senseless penny-pinching. I am, however, saying that there is no excuse for waste or unnecessary expenditures if one is faced with heavy competition. In any all-out business battle to capture markets, it is necessary to reduce all costs wherever possible—an axiom some firms and individuals tend to forget during peak boom periods.

Young men who want to start making a million today have a wide variety of business fields from which to choose when selecting their careers. The one an individual selects will, of course, depend largely on his particular talents, interest, background, training and experience. The alert manufacturer knows that there is a great demand for new and improved products of all kinds. The man with a flair for merchandising will see the great potentials in wholesaling or retailing. Other men will realize they can make their fortunes by providing new and better services to industry or the public at large. Simply stated, it all adds up to this: The man who comes up with a means for doing or producing almost anything better, faster or more economically has his future and his fortune at his fingertips. Don't misunderstand me. It is not easy to build a business and make a million. It takes hard—extremely hard—work. There are no nine-to-five hours and no five-day weeks for the boss.

"I studied the lives of great men and famous women," ex-President Harry S. Truman remarked, "and I found that the men and women who got to the top were those who did the jobs they had in hand, with everything they had of energy and enthusiasm and hard work."

There are no absolutely safe or sure-fire formulas for achieving success in business. Nonetheless, I believe that there are some fundamental rules to the game which, if followed, tip the odds for success very much in the businessman's favor. These are rules which I've applied throughout my entire career—and which every millionaire businessman with whom I am acquainted has followed. The rules have worked for them—and for me. They'll work for you, too.

1. Almost without exception, there is only one way to make a great deal of money in the business world—and that is in one's own business. The man who wants to go into business for himself should choose a field which he knows and understands. Obviously, he can't know everything there is to know from the very beginning, but he should not start until he has acquired a good, solid working knowledge of the business.

2. The businessman should never lose sight of the central aim of all business—to produce more and better goods or provide more and better services to more people at lower cost.

3. A sense of thrift is essential for success in business. The businessman must discipline himself to practice economy wherever possible, in his personal life as well as his business affairs. "Make your money first—then think about spending it," is the best of all possible credos for the man who wishes to succeed.

4. Legitimate opportunities for expansion should never be ignored or overlooked. On the other hand, the businessman must always be on his guard against the temptation to overexpand or launch expansion programs blindly, without sufficient justification and planning. Forced growth can be fatal to any business, new or old.

5. A businessman must run his own business. He cannot expect his employees to think or do as well as he can. If they could, they would not be his employees. When "The Boss" delegates authority or responsibility, he must maintain close and constant supervision over the subordinates entrusted with it.

6. The businessman must be constantly alert for new ways to improve his products and services and increase his production and sales. He should also use prosperous periods to find the ways by which techniques may be improved and costs lowered. It is only human for people to give little thought to economies when business is booming. That, however, is just the time when the businessman has the mental elbow room to examine his operations calmly and objectively and thus effect important savings without sacrificing quality

or efficiency. Many businessmen wait for lean periods to do these things and, as a result, often hit the panic button and slash costs in the wrong places.

7. A businessman must be willing to take risks—to risk his own capital and to lose his credit and risk borrowed money as well when, in his considered opinion, the risks are justified. But borrowed money must always be promptly repaid. Nothing will write finis to a career faster than a bad credit rating.

8. A businessman must constantly seek new horizons and untapped or under-exploited markets. As I've already said at some length, most of the world is eager to buy American products and know-how; today's shrewd businessman looks to foreign markets.

9. Nothing builds confidence and volume faster or better than a reputation for standing behind one's work or products. Guarantees should always be honored—and in doubtful cases, the decision should always be in the customer's favor. A generous service policy should also be maintained. The firm that is known to be completely reliable will have little difficulty filling its order books and keeping them filled.

10. No matter how many millions an individual amasses, if he is in business he must always consider his wealth as a means for improving living conditions everywhere. He must remember that he has responsibilities toward his associates, employees, stockholders—and the public.

Do you want to make a million? Believe me, you can— if you are able to recognize the limitless opportunities and potentials around you and will apply these rules and work hard. For today's alert, ambitious and able young men, all that glitters truly *can* be gold.

THE
MILLIONAIRE
MENTALITY

Luck, knowledge, hard work—especially hard work—a man needs them all to become a millionaire. But, above all, he needs what can be called "the millionaire mentality": that vitally aware state of mind which harnesses all of an individual's skills and intelligence to the tasks and goals of his business.

I once hired a man—call him George Miller, it's close enough—to superintend operations on some oil properties I owned outside Los Angeles, California. He was an honest, hardworking individual. He knew the oil business. His salary was commensurate with the responsibilities of his position, and he seemed entirely satisfied with both his job and the pay he received. Yet, whenever I visited the properties and inspected the drilling sites, rigs and producing wells, I invariably noted things I felt were being done in wrong or inefficient ways.

There were too many people on the payroll and there weren't adequate controls over costs. Certain types of work were being done too slowly; others were being performed too rapidly and hence without proper care. Some equipment items were being overstocked while there were shortages of others.

As for George Miller himself, I felt he was spending too much time doing administrative work in the Los Angeles office and not enough out in the field—on the drilling sites and rigs. Consequently, he wasn't able to exercise the necessary degree of direct personal supervision over the operations that were his responsibility.

All these things served to keep costs high, to slow production and hold down profits. But I liked Miller and was certain that he possessed all the qualifications of a top-notch superintendent. After some weeks, I had a man-to-man talk with him. I informed George bluntly that I thought there was considerable room for improvement in the manner in which he was handling his job.

"It's funny, but I need only to spend an hour on one of the sites and I spot several things we could do better or cheaper and increase production and profits," I told him. "Frankly, I can't understand why you don't see them, too."

"But you *own* the properties," the superintendent declared. "You have a direct personal interest in everything that happens on or to them. That's enough to sharpen any man's eyes to ways of saving—and thereby making—more money."

Truth to tell, I'd never thought of it in quite that way before. I mulled over what George said for several days and then decided to try an experiment. I had another talk with Miller.

"Look, George. Suppose I farm the properties out to you," I suggested. "Instead of paying you a salary, I'll give you a percent of the profits. The more efficient our operations, the bigger those profits will be—and the more money you'll make."

Miller gave the proposition some thought and then accepted the offer enthusiastically.

The change was immediate—and little short of miraculous. As soon as George realized that he, too, had a "direct personal interest" in the properties he really hit his stride. No longer merely a salaried employee, the superintendent became keenly concerned with cutting costs, boosting production and increasing the profits in which he was to share. He viewed operations on the drilling and well sites in an entirely different light, instantly recognizing—and correcting—faults which had theretofore eluded him. Miller shucked unnecessary personnel from the payroll, pared operating expenses to the bone and used his considerable native ingenuity to devise better methods for getting the work done. Where he'd previously spent two and sometimes three days each week in the Los Angeles office, he now made only brief appearances there once or twice a month and chafed impatiently until he could return to the drilling sites.

I inspected my properties again some 60 days after George

Miller took over under the new relationship. I checked the operations minutely, but could find nothing wrong. Indeed, I noted little if anything I could have improved upon personally. Needless to say, in a very short time both Miller and I were making far more money than we had before he started working on a profit-sharing basis. The incident taught me one of the many lessons which have led me to believe that most men fall into one of four general categories.

In the first group are those individuals who work best when they work entirely for themselves—when they own and operate their own businesses. Such men do not want to be employed by anyone. Their desire is to be completely independent. They care nothing for the security a salaried job offers. They want to create their own security and build their own futures entirely on their own. In short, they want to be their own bosses and are willing to accept the responsibilities and risk this entails.

Next are the men who, for any of a large number of reasons, do not want to go into business for themselves, but who achieve the best, and sometimes spectacular, results when they are employed by others and share in the profits of the business. There are many widely different types of men in this category. They range from topflight salesmen who prefer working on a commission basis—earning in proportion to what they produce, with neither floors nor ceilings on their incomes—to the finest executives in the business world.

George Miller was one who fit into this category. So— at the uppermost end of the scale—did the late Charles E. "Engine Charlie" Wilson. I'm certain that Charles E. Wilson would have achieved great success had he gone into business for himself. But he preferred working for someone else—first for the Westinghouse Electric Company and then for the General Motors Corporation. Wilson's rise from an 18-cent-an-hour job to the $600,000-a-year presidency of General Motors is a classic saga of American business. Charles E. Wilson was always an *employee*—but he amassed millions through stock-ownership in the companies for which he worked, thus sharing in the profits he helped to create.

My third category includes individuals who want only to be salaried employees, people who are reluctant to take risks and who work best when they are employed by others and enjoy the security of a steady salary. People in this group are good, conscientious and reliable workers. They are loyal to their employers, but are content with the limited incentives of a regular paycheck and hopes for occasional raises in salary. They do not possess the initiative and independence—and, perhaps, the self-confidence and drive—of individuals in the first two groups.

Lastly, there are those who work for others but have the same attitude toward their employers that postal clerks have toward the Post Office Department. I hasten to make clear that I intend no slight or slur against postal clerks, who work hard and well. But they are not motivated by any need or desire to produce a profit for their employer. Postal deficits are traditional and they are met regularly by the Federal Government. I doubt very seriously if there is one postal clerk in ten who cares whether the Post Office Department makes a profit or operates at a deficit. This is, perhaps, as it should be—in the Post Office Department. But, obviously, such attitudes are fatal to any business operating in a free-enterprise system.

Yet there are far too many men who hold—or would like to hold—management positions in business whose outlooks are virtually identical with those of the average postal clerk. They don't really care whether the company that employs them makes a profit or shows a loss as long as their own paychecks arrive on time.

I've encountered countless specimens—graduates of the nation's leading schools of business administration among them—who, incredibly enough, are utterly incapable of reading a balance sheet and couldn't even give an intelligent definition of what is meant by the term "profits." Whatever exalted titles such men may hold, they still remain nothing more than glorified postal clerks. They feel little or no sense of responsibility to their employers or the stockholders of the company for which they work. They are interested solely in their own personal welfare. Outwardly, some of these men seem to possess the essential qualifications for management jobs. They are obviously intelligent and apparently experienced. But not even a 180 I.Q. will necessarily make an individual a good businessman or executive. And, as Roger Falk so correctly points out in his book, *The Business of Management,* many a man who is supposed to have, say, ten years' experience has really had only one years' experience repeated ten times over.

Large numbers of these postal clerk types spend years— even decades—trying to reach the upper rungs of the success ladder and wondering why they can't attain them. They can't understand why they aren't given top jobs or can't "get rich."

The reason they fail? Actually, it's all in the mind.

Like it or not, there is a thing that can be called The Millionaire Mentality. There is a frame of mind which puts an individual a long way ahead on the road to success in business, whether it be in his own or as an executive. In short, The Millionaire Mentality is one which is always and above all cost-conscious and profit-minded. It is most likely to be found among men in the first two categories I have cited. This Millionaire Mentality is rarely found among individuals in the third group. But then, they seldom have ambitions to be anything more than employees in the lower or middle echelons of a business organization. The Millionaire Mentality is entirely nonexistent among men in the fourth category. Unfortunately, however, these are usually the very people who have the wildest delusions about their own value —the ones who do the least and demand the most. They view the company for which they work as a cornucopia from which good things should flow to them rather than as something to which they owe loyalty and which they should strive to build.

There were times in the past when I tried to excuse the failings of these types on the ground that they hadn't had the advantages I'd enjoyed in life. I reasoned that they did not have the same amount of formal education I'd received, hadn't traveled as widely nor had as much business experience as I. Then I gradually learned that when their personal interests were involved, these economic illiterates suddenly became as shrewd as the most successful financier.

I once took control of a company which had great potentials but a very disappointing earnings record. It didn't take me very long to pinpoint the trouble. Three of the company's key executives were virtually casebook examples of the postal clerk, men who were neither cost-conscious nor profit-minded.

Their monthly salaries ran into four figures. One month, shortly before payday, I instructed the accounting department to "short" each of their paychecks by five dollars—and, if they complained, to send them directly to me.

As I more or less expected, all three of the executives concerned presented themselves at my office within an hour after their checks were delivered on payday. To each, in turn, I delivered a little speech that was hardly calculated to brighten his day.

"I've been going over the company's books," I announced sourly. "I've found several examples of what I consider unnecessary expenditures which have cost this company's stockholders many tens of thousands of dollars in the last year. Apparently, you paid little or no attention to them. Certainly, I've seen no evidence that you tried to reduce the expenses or correct the situations which caused them to rise as high as they did. Yet, when your own paycheck is involved, you instantly notice a five-dollar underpayment and take immediate steps to have the mistake rectified." Two of the executives got the point, took it to heart and quickly mended their ways. The third did none of these things—and was soon looking elsewhere for work.

It should go without saying that no business can long survive unless it makes a profit. It should also go without saying that businessmen and business executives must be constantly alert for ways to reduce costs and increase efficiency, production, quality and sales so that the company he owns—or for which he works—can operate at a profit. These would appear to be the most basic of all basic business axioms. Yet it is a sad fact that many businessmen and executives barely comprehend them—and there are even those who don't comprehend them at all!

An all-too-familiar attitude was expressed to me recently by a young executive who complained bitterly that his departmental budget had been slashed by $20,000.

"Did the cut reduce the efficiency of your department or curtail any of its productive operations?" I asked him.

"No, I guess not," he replied after a moment's thought.

"Then why complain?" I inquired.

"We could have found *something* to spend the money on!" was this alleged executive's answer. "After all, you have to think big and spend money to make money!"

I'm glad this young man wasn't on one of my payrolls. I would have disliked terminating our conversation by firing him on the spot.

I've heard this concept that "you have to think big and spend money to make money" bandied about ever since I began my own business career. I doubt if there is any other business concept more widely misinterpreted. I agree that anyone who desires to achieve success and wealth in business must have imagination and be farsighted. He must also be willing to spend—and risk—money, but only when the expenditure is justified and the risk is carefully calculated to be worth it.

In my opinion, it's more important for the man with The Millionaire Mentality to be able to think small than to think big—in the sense that he gives meticulous attention to even the smallest details and misses no opportunity to reduce costs in his own or his employer's business. I explained my views along these lines not long ago to a newly graduated aspirant for a junior-executive position.

"Do you mean that a man has to be a penny pincher to be a success?" he wanted to know.

I replied that what might seem to be penny-pinching at one level might well loom as a large-scale economy at another. I mentioned the example of the giant U.S. corporation that recently made a study of the contents of the wastebaskets in its administrative offices.

Each night for a week, a team of workers emptied the waste receptacles and sorted out the usable items of company property which had been tossed into them by the firm's employees during the day. By computing the value of such minor items as paper clips, rubber bands, erasers, pencils, and so on which had been discarded during the week and multiplying the total by 52, company officials discovered that more than $30,000 was being wasted—literally thrown away—each year!

Another firm operating a fleet of trucks saved $15,000 annually on its gasoline bills just because an alert executive noticed that drivers were filling their fuel tanks to overflowing at the company gas pumps and that gasoline remaining in hose nozzles was allowed to drip onto the ground.

In one of my own companies, a bright junior executive burned much midnight oil to devise a shortcut in a production operation which saved less than a half a cent per unit, but added up to a total yearly saving of over $25,000—more than twice his own salary. Last year, he also reduced over-all costs by 20 percent and increased production by 12 percent in his own department, This young man quite definitely has what I term The Millionaire Mentality. He is, incidentally, no longer a *junior* executive. I do not hesitate to predict that he will reach the top and make his millions in record time.

In this day and age, almost every business firm has to fight a constant battle against rising costs. More than ever before in history, the emphasis has to be on reducing costs and increasing production. There is absolutely no room in today's business world for even the most junior executive who has a postal clerk's outlook—but there is an insatiable and ever-growing need for executives who possess or will develop Millionaire Mentalities. Faced with spiraling costs and shrinking profit margins, many firms have begun to weed out the former and give greater latitude and opportunity to the latter.

In my own companies, we have instituted a program of "early retirement" to rid ourselves of the personnel deadwood which has been allowed to collect over the years—and which, inevitably, collects in almost any business firm. Several hundred executives and employees have been compulsorily retired well before reaching the normal retirement age. The criterion for selecting those to be retired has been their actual value to the companies. In brief, the question asked in each case was whether the individual was productive, cost-conscious and profit-minded.

True, the cost of retiring these people and of paying them pensions years before they were due to receive them is very high. But we have found that the cost is significantly less than the cost of keeping them on our payrolls, where they not only draw full pay, but cause more harm than good, producing losses instead of profits.

The man with a Millionaire Mentality is not a penny

pincher and money-grubber. If he is an executive, he watches costs and tries to reduce them—and strives to increase production and sales and thus profits—in every way he can because he has the interests of the company, its shareholders and employees at heart. He knows that the healthier the company, the better its profit picture, the more those shareholders and employees will benefit.

It is more than a figure of speech to say that an executive holds the stockholders' investments and the employees' jobs in his trust. To discharge those trusts, he must direct every effort to insure that the company makes a fair profit—one not only large enough for it to continue in business, but also large enough for it to take advantage of opportunities for expansion. An executive who understands this and acts accordingly is already well on his way to establishing the frame of mind that produces The Millionaire Mentality.

PART TWO

How to Succeed in Business
by Really Trying

WHAT
MAKES AN
EXECUTIVE?

As part of a university survey designed to gauge their understanding of business theories and practices, several hundred entering freshmen recently were asked this question:

"Assuming that you owned a large business firm, what is the principal quality, trait or qualification you would want your executives to possess?"

Among the answers were these random—but fairly typical—examples:

"I'd want my executives to dress well and have good personalities."

"They would have to know how to entertain important customers."

"I'd only hire executives who could keep prices up and wages down."

"I'd insist on getting executives who were able to make people work harder and faster."

Now, naïve as these replies may sound, one cannot blame freshmen for being somewhat hazy about what goes on in the business world. Unfortunately, their ignorance is shared by far too many who are much older and should be much wiser. The principles of management personnel selection are often misunderstood, even by some who have long been active in the management of businesses. I have encountered more than a few supposedly experienced businessmen whose concepts of the qualities and qualifications they or other management personnel should possess are nearly as muddled as those of the students.

Take, for example, the pompous—and obviously job-seeking—executive who cornered me recently at a cocktail party. He complained bitterly that he had been passed over for promotion twice by the well-known firm for which he worked.

"I'm a victim of company politics," he declared, obviously believing it. "There's no other explanation. I've always performed my duties exactly as an executive should!"

"And how is that?" I inquired, my curiosity to hear what weird theories he'd propound getting the better of my good judgment.

"I keep a tight rein on the people in my department. I never let them put anything over on me or the company. If they try, I fire them on the spot!" the man replied with smug pride. "I don't question my orders and always carry them out to the letter, regardless of the consequences."

At this point, I suddenly pretended that I'd just recognized a long-lost relative across the room, disengaged myself and beat a rapid retreat. I'd heard all I cared to hear—or could stomach.

I can readily understand why this so-called executive hadn't been promoted. What I can't understand is why he hadn't been given the sack long before. Certainly, he wouldn't remain on my payroll for five minutes. He personifies the two worst qualities anyone holding down a responsible managerial job in a modern business firm could possibly possess. His attitude toward his subordinates is clearly that of a slave-driving martinet. His attitude toward his superiors—at least to their faces—is just as clearly that of a complete bootlicker utterly devoid of imagination or common sense.

Let's look at it this way. Business management may be broadly defined as the art of directing human activities so as to carry out a business firm's policies and achieve its goals. Whether it be general or specialized management—such as personnel, purchasing, production or sales—the key to all business management lies in the words: *directing human activities*.

No one possessing the attitudes of the disgruntled executive I met at the cocktail party could possibly *direct* human beings in any activity. His type can only drive or bully those unfortunate enough to work under him. It is hardly necessary to point out that these are not methods to which employees will respond favorably or by which they can be prevailed upon to work productively.

But our horrible example's managerial failings do not end there. His straight-faced avowal that he doesn't question his orders and always carries them out "to the letter, regardless of the consequences," brands him a toady. It also proves him to be an extremely stupid person who has no concept of the responsibilities every executive owes to his superiors and the company for which he works.

True, an executive should conscientiously and loyally carry out the instructions he receives from those above him. But this does not mean he should carry them out blindly, like some mindless automation. If he is a good executive, it follows that he will give careful consideration to "the consequences."

However exalted his position, no man is infallible. Even board chairmen are human, and thus liable to make mistakes. An alert junior executive who recognizes errors, fallacies or weaknesses in the orders he receives from his superiors and fails to call their attention to them is not being conscientious or loyal. He is simply shirking his responsibility.

Any seasoned top-level executive would much rather have his mistakes pointed out to him early by a subordinate than have those mistakes make themselves painfully apparent later in the company's profit and loss statement.

Years ago, I had to make some far-reaching decisions regarding the operations of one of my American companies. I was in Europe at the time and had received what I thought were all the needed facts in the form of letters, memoranda and reports from the company's management personnel. I didn't know, however, that a last-minute vitally important statistical report—which drastically amended all such reports previously sent from the U.S.—had been lost in the mails. The report did not reach me, and thus, I unwittingly based my planning on incomplete information.

Arriving at what I considered were the correct decisions, I sent an instruction letter to the company's offices in the United States. A few days later, I received an urgent transatlantic telephone call from one of the firm's executives. He politely but firmly pointed out that I'd apparently failed to take certain important facts into consideration, and that if the program I'd outlined were implemented, the company would suffer heavy losses.

After talking at what seemed to be cross-purposes for several minutes, we both realized I had based some key calculations on outdated statistical information. A copy of the missing report was airmailed to me immediately and I revised my calculations, decisions and instructions.

The program I finally outlined eventually proved successful and profitable—thanks to the alertness of this company-management executive. I hate to think what the results would have been if all the firm's executives were the kind who never questioned their orders and carried them out "to the letter, regardless of the consequences!"

Naturally, I—like everyone else who owns or controls businesses—have a great interest in management personnel selection. I believe there are certain universally applicable criteria by which a business executive's potential value to a company may be weighed.

I don't pretend that my personal yardsticks are infallible, but they are very similar to those used by a great many other successful businessmen, and they have proved fairly accurate through the years. Much of my own business success is due to my executives' loyalty and efficiency; thus I think it reasonable to assume that the criteria by which they were chosen and promoted are reliable.

How do I judge whether or not a man is—or would be—a good executive? I hold that the first acid test of an executive is his ability to think and act for himself. He should have the intelligence and ability to originate ideas, develop plans, implement programs, solve problems and meet situations without running constantly to his superiors for advice. In my opinion, a man who cannot do these things is not an executive. He is a glorified office boy.

Once, when I asked a leading American industrialist how he visualized the perfect management team, he conjured up the following picture of a businessman's nirvana:

"My executives would be men I could call into my office at nine A.M. on January first and tell them: 'Look, boys, the company has been making sausage skins for years. Last year, our profit was a million dollars. This year, I've decided that we stop making sausage skins and start turning out nuts and bolts.'

"At that, all the executives would smile, nod and file out of my office. I wouldn't see them again until five P.M. on December thirty-first. Then, they'd come back into my office to tell me we were producing the world's finest nuts and bolts, underselling our competitors by fifty percent—and had tripled our profits over the previous year!"

Of course, the industrialist's happy pipe dream was just that—a pipe dream. But it serves to illustrate the point I'm trying to make. A good executive is a man who can think and act independently and needs only the barest minimum of instruction to carry out his job.

Now, an executive's principal duty is to direct the activities—the work—of those under him. Direction being nothing less than another word, leadership, it follows that the good executive must, perforce, think and act as a leader.

Unfortunately, very few men are natural-born leaders. There is only one Churchill to a generation. But most intelligent, willing men can acquire or develop traits and qualities of leadership adequate to most situations they are likely to encounter in their careers.

As for the men who become business executives, some learn their lessons in leadership at college, others on their jobs, yet others in company-operated management-training courses. There are, of course, some who never learn—but they are very much in the minority and seldom climb very high on any business-management ladder.

Wherever it may be that an individual obtains his lessons in leadership, he learns certain basic rules which apply with equal validity in a business firm or on a battlefield. If followed, they go a very long way toward qualifying any man for a position of leadership. Among them are these five which I, personally, consider especially important:

What Makes an Executive?

1. Example is the best means to instruct or inspire others. The man who shows them as well as tells them is the one who gets the most from his surbordinates.

2. A good executive accepts full responsibility for the actions of the people under him. If called before his superiors because something has gone wrong in his department or office, he accepts full personal blame, for the fault is his for having exercised poor supervision.

3. The best leader never asks anyone under him to do anything he is unable—or unwilling—to do himself.

4. The man in charge must be fair but firm with his subordinates, showing concern for their needs and doing all he can to meet their reasonable requests. He treats his juniors with patience, understanding and respect and backs them to the hilt. On the other hand, he does not pamper them, and always bears in mind that familiarity breeds contempt.

5. There is one seemingly small—but actually very important—point that all executives should remember. Praise should always be given in public, criticism should always be delivered in private. Employees who have done a good job should be told so in front of their fellows; this raises morale all around. Employees who have done something wrong should be told so in private: otherwise, they will be humiliated and morale will drop.

I learned my own lessons in leadership many years ago in the tough, no-nonsense school provided by the oil fields. Virtually all the wildcatting operators—including me—knew the jobs of every man in our prospecting and drilling crews. We never asked a man to do anything we would not—or could not—do ourselves. Wherever possible, we showed our men what we wanted done and how we wanted them to do it.

"The best boss is one who knows the business better than I do, but trusts me—even though he never lets me forget that he's the boss," an old-time rigger once told me. "That's the kind of man I'll really work my tail off for . . ."

I think that basically every employee feels much the same way. Although few of today's executives are out in the field, sweating alongside their work crews, the old, tried-and-proved rules still hold. I believe that the most successful executives are those who follow them implicitly.

Yet another quality I seek in management personnel is the ability to communicate. Time is money in business; misunderstandings in the interpretation of requests, reports or instructions can prove very costly. Thus, the good executive is one who can explain things and tell people what needs to be done quickly and clearly.

Interest and enthusiasm are two more qualities a good executive must possess. No man can properly do a job in which he is not interested. An executive's interest must go far beyond the limits of his own particular department or office. It is essential that he know what goes on in other departments and that he be completely conversant with the company's policies and over-all activities. Only thus can he evaluate the role and relative efficiency of his department and relate its operations as a functioning part of a functioning whole to the other parts and to the whole itself.

Then, his interest should go even further: to embrace the entire field or industry in which his company operates. Only if he knows the field can he understand his company's strengths, weaknesses and problems.

But interest alone is not enough. There must also be a strong element of enthusiasm in his attitude. I hardly mean any hip, hip, hooray! variety of enthusiasm. I've never gone along with the school of thought that calls for sales meetings to open with rousing company songs. What I do mean is that an executive should thoroughly like his work. He should—starting with the operations of his own department —actively seek ways whereby his firm's efficiency, production, sales and profits may be increased.

Loyalty—another important quality in executives—can only be recognized and judged after it has been demonstrated. The executive's loyalty should not be to any individual—but to the stockholders, employees, his associates, superiors and the company as a whole.

These, then, are the characteristics which I believe are the most important for business executives to possess. Doubtless, some readers will be surprised by the fact that I've left out such things as personality, education and technical knowledge. But, on closer analysis, it should become clear that these are not really as basic or important as those qualities I have mentioned.

What Makes an Executive?

I'll agree that an individual with a completely negative personality can hardly expect to achieve success in any position which calls for him to work with people. On the other hand, an executive's job is to run his department, not to run in a popularity contest.

As for education, it depends largely on how one is using the term. I've found there are many top-quality business executives whose formal education stopped at high school or even grade school. What they know, they taught themselves. There is much knowledge a good executive should possess, but he does not necessarily have to obtain it at a college or university. Although a good, solid formal education is usually a great help to a man who wants to be a good executive, I don't believe that it is always essential.

Technical knowledge? I'll admit that in this day of complex industrial and business technology, every executive needs a greater degree of technical knowledge. But the kind and amount depends largely on what he is doing and where he is doing it. I can sum up my views on the subject by saying that I'd rather try to make a good technician out of a good executive who has no technical knowledge than try to make a good executive out of a good technician who has no executive ability.

Among other traits I imagine most laymen would list as being desirable in executives are such things as honesty, industry and imagination. I have purposely omitted these and several others because I consider them to be self-evident and think it is superfluous to mention them. Certainly, no businessman in his right mind would ever hire an executive if he had the least suspicion that the man was dishonest, lazy or unimaginative.

There's really no magic or secret to being a good executive. I think any man who has the qualities I've listed, sincerely wants a business career and will work and apply himself can become a good executive. Such a man would most certainly fit most successful businessmen's requirements for management personnel. He would most certainly fit into almost any firm in almost any industry. In my opinion, his career would be assured. He would, in short, have it made in the business world.

THE
FORCE OF
HABIT

There was a time when I was a fairly heavy cigarette smoker. Then, several years ago, I was on a vacation and motoring through France. One day, after driving for hours through some particularly foul rainy weather, I stopped for the night at a hotel in a small town in the Auvergne. Tired after the long and difficult drive, I had dinner and went up to my room. I undressed, got into bed and quickly fell asleep.

For some reason, I awoke about two A.M., acutely aware that I wanted a cigarette. Switching on the light, I reached for the cigarette package I'd placed on the nightstand before retiring. It proved to be empty. Annoyed—but still wanting a cigarette—I got out of bed and searched the pockets of the clothes I had been wearing. The search proved fruitless, and I went on to grope through my luggage in hopes that I might have accidentally left a pack of cigarettes in one of my suitcases. Again I was disappointed. I knew the hotel bar and restaurant had closed long before and guessed that it would be worse than useless to summon the crotchety night porter at such an hour. The only way I could hope to obtain any cigarettes was by dressing and then going to the railroad station, which was located at least six blocks away.

The prospect was not very pleasant. The rain still pelted down outside. My car was garaged a considerable distance from the hotel and, in any event, I had been warned the garage closed at midnight and did not reopen until six o'clock in the morning. The chances of getting a taxi were nil.

All in all, it was clear that if I was to have the cigarette I wanted so badly, I would have to walk to the railroad station—and back—through the pouring rain. But the desire to smoke gnawed at me and, perversely, the more I contemplated the difficulties entailed in getting a cigarette, the more desperately I wanted to have one. And so I took off my pajamas and started putting on my clothes. I was completely dressed and reaching for my raincoat when I abruptly stopped and began to laugh—at myself. It had suddenly struck me that my actions were illogical, even ludicrous.

There I stood, a supposedly intelligent human being, a supposedly responsible and fairly successful businessman who considered himself sensible enough to give other people orders. Yet I was ready to leave my comfortable hotel room in the middle of the night and slosh a dozen blocks through a driving rainstorm for no other reason than that I wanted a cigarette—because I felt that I "had" to have one.

For the first time in my life, I was brought face to face with the realization that I had developed a habit so strong that I was willing—automatically and unthinkingly—to let myself in for a very great deal of personal discomfort merely to satisfy it. Instead of simply enjoying the pleasure of an occasional smoke, I'd allowed myself to form a habit that had grown completely out of hand and was obviously operating contrary to my best interests, producing no commensurately beneficial results. Suddenly sharply aware of this, I rebelled mentally. I needed only a moment to arrive at a decision. I considered it an excellent idea—and an ideal time and place—to rid myself of a habit that was certainly doing me no good.

Having made up my mind, I took the empty cigarette packet that still lay on the nightstand, crumpled it up and tossed it into the wastebasket. Then I undressed, once more put on my pajamas and got back into bed. It was with a sense of relief—even of triumph—that I switched off the light, closed my eyes and listened to the rain beating against the windows of the room. In a few minutes, I drifted off into a sound and contented sleep. I haven't smoked a cigarette— nor have I felt any desire to smoke one—since that night.

Now, I do not intend any of this as an indictment of either cigarettes or smoking. I recount the anecdote solely to show how, in my own case, a habit got out of control to the extent that it controlled me, rather than the other way around.

Practices do become habits—and the force of those habits can, indeed, be mighty. However, human beings have a considerable degree of latitude. They are, after all, endowed with the ability to form their own habits and to break or discard those which they find undesirable.

Nowhere do habit patterns count for as much, and nowhere does the force of habit demonstrate its might more emphatically than in the business world. A businessman's habits are among the most important factors that determine whether he will be a success—or a failure.

For instance, it is a helpful habit for a businessman to be optimistic and enthusiastic. It will make his own work better and easier and will also serve to hearten and inspire his associates and subordinates. However, habitual optimism and enthusiasm can be carried to dangerous—and even disastrous—extremes of overestimation and overzealousness.

I recall the case of a brilliant and highly capable businessman—Bill Smith is as good a name for him as any—whose optimism helped him greatly in establishing and operating several manufacturing firms that showed good profits and great promise. Unfortunately, all of Bill Smith's business experience was obtained during a boom period. Consequently, his rosiest outlooks and hopes were always realized by developments in what was a steadily rising market.

Then, suddenly, there was a relatively mild economic recession. It was a time when seasoned businessmen pulled in their horns somewhat, did a little retrenching and proceeded cautiously while they waited for the business situation to become stabilized.

Bill Smith was totally unable to adjust to what, for him, were new and unfamiliar conditions. His habits of optimism and enthusiasm were too deeply ingrained. Instead of applying his brakes, he continued to move at full speed, supremely confident that everything would turn out fine.

Within a very short time, Smith had bitten off far more than he could chew under the business conditions that then prevailed. He overextended himself and his companies and eventually went bankrupt.

The Force of Habit

It is the widespread custom to say that people "develop" good habits and "fall into" bad ones. The implication, of course, is that the former are difficult to achieve, that the individual must make a constant conscious effort to form them, while he will slide easily and effortlessly into the latter. This is true—but needlessly so and almost solely because of the perversity of human nature. Actually, a habit is a habit. There should be no valid reason why it is any more difficult to form good ones than bad.

For instance, I—along with a great many others—contend that promptness, or the lack of it, is largely a matter of habit. One either forms the good habit of being on time —or forms the bad habit of being chronically tardy.

It is to any individual's advantage and best interests to be prompt, whether it is in keeping an appointment, paying a debt, meeting an obligation or keeping a promise of any kind.

The habitually late dinner guest discommodes his hosts and the others who have been invited to the affair. He quickly becomes unpopular and, sooner or later, he is dropped from guest lists.

Habitual promptness is an especially valuable asset for any businessman. That ancient adage "Time is money" has always been valid and it is more valid today than ever before. The pace and complexity of contemporary business place a premium on every hour and minute. Businessmen and executives must run their workdays on the tightest of schedules. They cannot afford to waste their productive time any more than they can afford to have needless stoppages on the production line.

Witness the constantly increasing number of corporations that operate their own aircraft so that they can move their executives from one place to another faster—to get them wherever they must go on time. There are more than 34,000 corporate aircraft in the United States today. General Motors, for example, maintains a fleet of 22 planes.

Montgomery Ward openly admits that the cost of flying its executives aboard its own aircraft is a third more than it would be to send them to their destinations on regular scheduled airline flights. But the use of corporate planes saves nearly 60 percent of the company executives' traveling time—and Montgomery Ward, like so many other companies, understands that the time saved is well worth the additional cost.

In short, the man who is where he said he would be at the time he promised to be there is not only making an excellent impression, he is saving—and thereby making—money for himself or for his company.

The need for promptness extends to every phase of business. The businessmen and firms most likely to succeed are those that fill their orders, deliver their merchandise, provide their services, pay their bills and meet their notes and other obligations on time. Customers who are made to wait for delivery on their orders beyond the promised time are likely to place their next orders elsewhere. Individuals and firms that pay their bills when they fall due establish good credit ratings—while those that lag behind soon find that it becomes extremely difficult or impossible for them to obtain credit anywhere.

Notwithstanding the countless advantages of habitual promptness, there are those who form the habit of being late regardless of the consequences. It is perversity, laziness and lack of foresight that cause an individual to form the habit of being tardy—just as it is these same factors that cause most people to form most of the habits that harm them and their business careers.

Thrift is another habit that can be formed—and that very often adds a deciding ingredient to any business success formula. Common sense should prove to any person that it is sound policy to economize wherever it is reasonably practicable to do so.

This holds true from the bottom up. Assume that a man wants to start in business for himself. In order to do this, he must have at least some capital, no matter what the business may be. In most cases, there are only three avenues open to him for obtaining that capital. He can provide it from his own savings, get it by taking in a partner or partners, or borrow it. If the money is his own from the start, the business, too, will be his own. If, however, he has to take in partners, he will own only part of the business and will have to share his profits. And, if he borrows money, the loan must be repaid—almost invariably with interest, which naturally reduces the profits.

Once he has started a business, an individual who is naturally thrifty will have an infinitely greater chance for success than another of equal ability who does not possess this quality. The habitually thrifty person will be able to immediately recognize opportunities for lowering overhead and production costs—and in present-day, highly competitive markets even minor savings can mean a great deal and even represent the difference between a net profit and a net loss.

Beyond this, the person who has formed thrifty habits will always have a fluid reserve to meet contingencies, carry him through slack periods or make it possible for him to expand or make improvements without resorting to borrowing.

The astute individual realizes that such habits as promptness and thrift can greatly help him achieve his goals. He practices promptness and thrift until they become second nature to him—and he reaps rewards from the beneficial force these habits exert on his career.

But these are by no means the only positive habits that can—and do—provide a powerful propellent to send a man to the top of the success ladder.

One of the most valuable habits any tyro businessman or executive can form is that of taking a last-minute pause to rapidly review his reasoning before he makes a decision. This final check-out may require only a few minutes or even a few seconds, but it pays large dividends. It provides the individual with one final—and priceless—opportunity to arrange his thoughts in logical order and to refresh his memory as to why and how he arrived at his decision. This simple procedure greatly increases the individual's ability to instantly and convincingly counter any objections that may arise. It is, in a way, analogous to the habit formed by many of the world's finest actors who, although they may know their part in a play thoroughly, will nonetheless give the script or at least their lines a quick skimming over before the curtain goes up for a performance.

One of the most successful salesmen I have ever known—he is now a top sales executive in a giant corporation—maintains that he owes much of his success to having formed this habit early in his career.

"I even developed a sort of personal gimmick to form the habit," he told me. "When calling on an account, I invariably stopped off first to have a cup of coffee, get a shoeshine or do something of the sort. This gave me a final chance to mentally review my presentation before actually setting foot in the customer's office. It worked wonders. I sold much more effectively and was always prepared to answer any questions or objections that arose."

There is no doubt about it—at least not in my mind: whether or not one needs a gimmick to do so, it is an excellent idea to form the habit of taking a last-minute mental breathing spell to organize one's thoughts before making decisions.

Another—albeit much less simple—habit that should be acquired by any man who wants to get ahead rapidly in business is the habit of being relaxed. The successful businessman is usually the one who is always relaxed—even in the face of adversity. Now, I hardly intend to imply that he is apathetic, indolent and lethargic. What I mean is that he keeps his mind receptive and responsive—always ready to grasp and exploit new opportunities and to understand and cope with new problems. He is poised, but never rigid and unyielding, in the face of changing situations.

The seasoned businessman is relaxed in the same sense that a crack football player is relaxed. The football player who intercepts a pass does not freeze or panic because the ball has unexpectedly fallen into his hands. The new situation that has suddenly developed does not leave him immobile. His reactions are flexible enough to grasp and cope —and he takes a firm grip on the ball and runs with it, still alert and yet relaxed enough to shift direction and avoid opposing tacklers.

A few—a very few—fledgling businessmen have an innate ability to assume this sort of relaxed attitude even under great stress. But the vast majority of men in business form the habit through years of experience.

"Always think of yourself as a man who has just fallen overboard in the middle of a lake," a veteran oilman advised me early in my business career. "If you keep your wits about you, you can always swim to shore or at least dog-paddle or float until someone 'fishes you out. But if you lose your head—if you panic—you're finished!"

I suppose that a man starting out in the business world is, in a way, like one who suddenly finds himself in the middle of a lake. If he remains calm, his chances of survival are high. If he doesn't, he'll most probably drown. The tyro businessman and young executive should constantly bear this analogy in mind. It will do much to help them form the habit of being relaxed and thus able to handle themselves in any situation.

Obviously, it would be impossible to list every habit that is good or bad for every man in business. Far too much depends on the individual, his nature and personality, the particular field or type of business in which he is engaged and many other variable factors.

However, any individual—whether he is in business or not—can determine which habits are beneficial to him and which are harmful. Habits that help an individual live and work better and achieve his goals are, of course, good ones —habits that the individual should try to acquire or form. Those that harm or hinder, interfere or obstruct, serve no practical purpose or offer no positive results should be avoided or, if already formed, should be broken as quickly as possible.

Executives and businessmen would do well to periodically make a careful inventory of the things they do in connection with their work with sufficient regularity for them to assume the character of habits. It is a good idea to list these on a piece of paper. Then it is up to the individual to make his own evaluations of the habits he has listed. If he is honest with himself, he will readily recognize some of them as being bad. These he will do his energetic best to discard with a minimum of delay.

Next, there will be some habits that appear to fall into the "indifferent" or "undecided" category. These must be considered objectively to determine if they can be modified in order to make them positive.

For example, one executive I know had formed the habit of holding weekly staff meetings with all the employees in his department. Although the idea was basically sound, the meetings had been held for several months without producing any notably useful results.

The executive was almost convinced that he should discontinue the practice. Then, making a habit inventory, he gave considerable thought to the problem of why the meetings had been failures. Analyzing the matter, he finally hit upon the answer. He had been holding the staff meetings at 4:15 every Friday afternoon.

Human nature being what it is, the minds of the employees at that time each Friday were on going home for the weekend. They had little interest or enthusiasm for discussions of office matters 45 minutes before quitting time. The executive changed the time and the day of the week—and his habit of holding weekly office-staff meetings moved up into the good-habit category almost immediately. The meetings were thereafter productive of many ideas that improved output and efficiency and raised employee morale to a new high. But an indifferent habit that cannot be raised to the "good" category should be discarded, for if it is continued, it can only slide down into the "bad" classification.

As for those of his business habits that are clearly good, the astute businessman will strive to make them even more useful, advantageous and productive. For instance, if he can lay claim to being habitually thrifty, to being constantly on the alert for ways to cut costs and effect savings, he should determine to redouble his efforts—to find more ways of reducing expenses and thus increasing the company's profits.

The individual who wants to reach the top in business must appreciate the might of the force of habit—and must understand that practices are what create habits. He must be quick to break those habits that can break him—and hasten to adopt those practices that will become the habits that help him achieve the success he desires.

BUSINESS BLUNDERS
AND
BOOBY TRAPS

Every business executive is going to make mistakes in his career. The important thing is to learn from them—and avoid repetition. But there are certain recurring situations and procedures which seem to invite error and misjudgment. It is up to the alert executive to anticipate and evaluate these "traps." As for those blunders and errors of judgment which will inevitably occur, the same "millionaire" mentality which ensures success will survive *and* profit by them.

Like most people, I'd much prefer to have the memories of my mistakes fade quietly into oblivion, but there are many I cannot forget. Among them are three monumental blunders I shall always remember.

The first dates back to my days in the Oklahoma oil fields. Buying the oil lease on a property located in an area later known as the "Yale Pool," I hired a geologist to inspect the site and to recommend whether or not I should drill.

"There's no oil on the land," he reported. "The property is worthless. The best thing you can do is get rid of the lease!" I followed his advice and sold. A short time later, the Yale Pool proved to be a rich oil-producing area. I'd thrown away a fortune.

My second giant—but hardly economy-sized—blunder was made in 1931. Firms in which I already held substantial interests and I bought more than two million dollars' worth of Mexican Seaboard Oil Company common at prevailing Depression-era lows. Then, the stock market took another downturn. I was certain we'd made a safe and sound investment in Mexican Seaboard, but my fellow directors feared that the market would go even lower.

"We can't take any more risks," they argued. "We have

to unload." Outvoted, I finally went along with the majority. The firms—and I—sold our Mexican Seaboard stock.

Had we held the shares we already owned and bought more in 1931, we could have acquired control of the company at a fantastic bargain price. Mexican Seaboard common's subsequent performance proved that this would have been a major financial coup—and that I would have made millions.

I pulled my worst boner in 1932. I was interested in obtaining an oil concession in Iraq, where geological surveys and exploration operations indicated the presence of vast oil deposits beneath the hell-hot desert sands. My representative, conducting negotiations with Iraqi government officials in Baghdad, reported that a tempting concession was available for a price that could be tallied in tens of thousands of dollars. Just then, the U.S. crude-oil price broke; East Texas crude plummeted to ten cents a barrel—and the petroleum industry was in a panic. Fearing to risk capital outlays under those circumstances, I ordered my agent in Baghdad to halt all negotiations.

The next time I had an opportunity to buy a Middle Eastern oil concession, in 1949, I seized it unhesitatingly. Conditions were far different than they had been 17 years earlier, however. In 1949, I had to pay $12,500,000 in cash upon signing the concession agreement!

Bad as they were, it would be solacing to think these were my only errors, but I made many others and will doubtless make many more. As I've said before, businessmen are no exceptions to the rule that everyone makes mistakes. But personal experience and observation have taught me that most mistakes made by businessmen and executives fall into certain broad, though readily definable, categories.

Naturally enough, it is the young businessman who, through inexperience or immaturity, usually makes the most errors. Some of his blunders are inadvertent, not very serious and entirely understandable and excusable. Other errors are the results of inadequate training or insufficient or faulty understanding of business in general or of his own business in particular. Yet other blunders stem from out-and-out inaptitude or incompetence—but these, needless to say, soon prove fatal to any business career.

The examples I've cited from personal experience serve

to illustrate three of the major categories of mistakes I've found are most commonly and most often made by businessmen, especially when they are relatively inexperienced and unseasoned.

The first of these is the failure—or the inability—to distinguish between what is fact and what is opinion. Though it may be carefully considered and based on fact, opinion nonetheless remains opinion—and it is very seldom infallible. Opinion is never better than the information on which it is based, the qualifications of the person voicing it and his ability to correctly interpret the information at his disposal. Businessmen are sometimes inclined to read or hear opinions and accept them as facts upon which to base their plans or make their decisions without further investigation or study. Such was the error I made when I sold my lease on the Yale Pool property. Although I was well aware that in those days geology was far from being the most exact of sciences, I blindly accepted the word—the opinion—of the geologist who inspected the property. I did not take the time nor the trouble to consult anyone else to obtain a "cross-reading" on the single "expert's" judgment. I cannot blame the geologist for making a wrong recommendation. I can blame only myself for accepting it without question.

The predilection for accepting opinion or even rumor as fact is a fairly familiar and widespread human failing. Anyone harboring doubts on this score need only reflect on how often he has heard individuals repeat as fact the opinionated statements they read in highly biased newspaper editorials, gleaned from propaganda handouts of one kind or another or heard as rumors in the streets.

Remember the perennial tale of the leprous Chinese cook's thumb that turned up in a bowl of chow mein at the (usually local) chop suey parlor? That particular yarn was already hoary with age when I was a boy—yet it's still making the rounds, and it's still being given credence by the gullible. This, of course, is an extreme example, but businessmen frequently allow their judgment to be influenced by opinions and rumors which, in their own way, are no less factitious than this unappetizing fable. Many otherwise astute businessmen will buy or sell sizable blocks of stock merely because they "hear" that certain issues are "due" to go up or down on the Stock Exchange. Nine times out of ten, they find that they've done the wrong thing because they listened to opinions or rumors rather than determine the facts for themselves.

A short time ago, a manufacturer I know spent nearly $100,000 tooling up and buying the raw materials to produce a novelty item which, according to trade journal articles he'd read, was in great demand. Not until he was ready to go into production did he discover that half-a-dozen other firms were ahead of him and beginning to distribute the item. The market was saturated even before his salesmen could start selling his product. He was badly stuck. This could not have happened had he checked all the facts before leaping into a clearly stupid business situation.

There may be some substitute for hard facts and factual information, but if there is, I have no idea what it can be. It certainly isn't rumor or opinion that has been camouflaged as fact. In order to succeed in any "deal," project or endeavor, the businessman must assemble all the available pertinent hard facts and study and analyze them himself. There's nothing wrong in asking the opinions of others and in taking them into consideration. The mistake lies in accepting and following other people's advice blindly, in accepting their opinions without first determining if they are backed up by facts. This is one of the first lessons young businessmen and executives should learn—or they will find themselves being taught it the hard way!

Once satisfied that he has made a sound decision based on sound judgment of the facts, the businessman can plot the course whereby he will implement his decisions or programs. And, he should stick to that course and follow it through. The failure to do this is another of the blunders often made by young businessmen—and by some who are not so young.

That's where I made my big error in 1931. I did not have the courage of my convictions, and I failed to stick by my decisions and to my plans. I was convinced that Mexican Seaboard common was a good—an unusually good—investment. I had made careful, painstaking studies of the company's history, its organizational, financial and debt structure, its potential and all other conceivably pertinent factors. It was only after I'd done all this that I bought large blocks of Mexican Seaboard stock on my own account and used my influence to encourage the firms in which I held substantial interests to do likewise. When Mexican Seaboard shares dropped a few points, the directors of the boards on which I also sat became nervous and voted to sell out the firms' holdings. My arguments were unavailing, and the firms sold their Mexican Seaboard stock. Whereupon, instead of hewing to my original plans, I followed suit. I "dumped" my own shares. I suffered a considerable loss on my original investment, for the stock was selling for less than what I had paid for it. Far more serious was the loss of the very large potential profit that would have accrued to me in the ensuing years, when the stock multiplied many times in value, just as I had reasoned it would—as I knew from my careful studies of the company that it *must*.

This was a stock transaction. It is not difficult to find analogous situations in commerce and industry. Quite often, businessmen become frightened at the very first signs of slowdowns or setbacks after they have launched a well-planned and organized production or sales program. They hit the panic button and scrap the entire program, suffering heavy financial losses as a result. This is particularly true of un-seasoned men who do not have the calm, cool patience to wait until more returns come in nor the experience to understand that a redoubling of efforts or even some slight modification in plan might make the program a complete success, or at least carry it through to conclusion without loss.

It has always been my contention that if corporate books were kept properly, there would be a separate ledger in which accountants entered the dollars-and-cents costs of executives' and businessmen's errors and mistakes. Certainly, there would be few entries in such ledgers that would show up more glaringly than the cost of premature, defeatist cancellations of plans and programs already under way.

My 1932 bobble in turning down the Iraqi oil concession illustrates another blunder frequently made by businessmen —namely, their reluctance to take risks. A businessman has to be willing to take risks. They may be planned and calculated, but they're risks just the same. The shrewd business-man weighs all the known and, to his knowledge, possible factors in a given situation. He tries to allow for all the variables, but he is well aware that he cannot think of nor insure against every contingency. He accepts the idea that there is always a possibility that some completely unforeseen element or development will turn up to alter or even wreck his plans. He is, however, secure in the knowledge that he has done everything within his power to tip the odds for success in his own favor.

Obviously, I was not very shrewd in 1932. Had I stopped to reason things out, I would have realized that the crude-oil price-break was only a temporary problem, that the price of crude would have to go higher—much higher. I should have also realized that the demand for petroleum products would continue to increase throughout the years, and that it would be only a matter of time before the world would see a mad scramble as oil companies sought new sources of crude-oil production. Considering the bargain-basement price at which the Iraqi concession was being offered, the risks involved in buying it would have been more than offset by the potentials for eventual profit.

The businessman who is able to calculate his risks—and then is willing to take them—has his battle for success nine-tenths won. The remaining one-tenth is the unknown variable, the unpredictable factor that puts the zest and excitement into the game. Without that "x" factor, business would be hopelessly dull, routine and uninteresting.

Young businessmen and executives make other mistakes than those I've already discussed. Often, the fault is not theirs at all. Young men generally start out in the business world today as strictly disciplined and as passively obeisant as the novices of some pagan cult. By the time they leave their schools and colleges, where they receive overspecialized educations, they are virtually consecrated to the Moloch of "Organization" and dedicated to serving the complex rituals of memorandum and buck-passing. They are—and remain forever—cloistered from the unanointed laity of the rank-and-file production workers. The organization chart—the more complex the better—is their Grand Totem. Whole volumes—or preferably entire shelves—of procedural rules are their most honored fetishes. They are conditioned to meet periodically in solemn conclave and pore over the esoterica of statistical tables and committee reports. They are as far removed from the harsh, mundane realities of commerce and industry as Egyptian priests arguing abstruse theological doctrines in the sanctum of the inner temple.

I made my first million dollars in the front seat of a battered, secondhand Model T Ford. The flivver served as my executive office and field headquarters—sometimes even as my bedroom. I transacted enormous amounts of business and signed many important leases, contracts and agreements in the front seat of the mud-splattered tin lizzy. When it was necessary to have documents witnessed, one or two of my drillers or roustabouts scrawled their signatures on the papers, using the jalopy's wrinkled fenders as writing surfaces. There wasn't anything unusual about any of this. Almost every independent operator—the wildcatter—who prospected and drilled for oil during the early days in Oklahoma operated in much the same manner. He had no fixed hours, no five-day week. He had to be his own promoter, geologist, legal advisor, explosives expert, drilling superintendent and jack-of-all-trades. Most of his time was spent in the field, working alongside his men.

He often went for days without any sleep save for what naps he could take on the drilling rig or curled up in his automobile.

The wildcatter operated on a perpetually frayed shoe-string budget—at least until he brought in his first big producer. He constantly faced heavy competition; his business was fraught with innumerable financial perils and pitfalls; as a natural consequence, he developed certain traits and techniques and learned certain lessons which, I'm afraid, today's young businessmen have little opportunity to develop or learn.

We, the "independents," eliminated all unnecessary administrative overhead expenses in our operations. We scorned renting offices in the boom towns that burgeoned around the oil fields, partly because we didn't want to spend the extra money on what we considered an unnecessary frill, but mainly because we knew that it was impossible to run our operations properly from behind a desk. We familiarized ourselves thoroughly with all aspects of our business and kept all our costs down by exercising unceasing and vigilant supervision over every phase of our operations. We often worked employee-morale and production miracles by donning overalls and sweating and grunting along with our men even on the toughest and dirtiest jobs.

It wasn't until I'd brought in a few producing wells that I thought to trade my Model T for a new Dodge and to rent desk space in someone else's Tulsa office. By then, I was worth a million dollars—on paper. Nonetheless, I still wore work clothes more often than I did business suits. I was running three strings of rotary tools—drilling three wells—simultaneously and acting as my own financial manager, purchasing agent, tool-pusher and drilling superintendent. There were often times when I'd work around several clocks without sleep to keep things moving on the drilling sites.

Is this boasting? I think not; as I've said, most independent operators worked the same way. Bill and Charles Roeser, R. M. McFarlin, George Forman, Josh Cosden, Bill Skelly—these were only a few of the countless others who retained their basic outlooks and attitudes toward business even after they'd made their million or millions.

What I'm trying to point out with all this are some of the differences between the businessmen of that era and those of today. I'm also attempting to point up what I consider some of the glaring errors made by today's young businessmen and, for that matter, by American business firms and American business as a whole.

First of all, there is the attitude toward administrative overhead. Years ago, businessmen automatically kept administrative overhead to an absolute minimum. The present-day trend is in exactly the opposite direction. The modern business mania is to build greater and ever greater paper-shuffling empires. Many business firms employ battalions of superspecialized executives, reinforce them with regiments of office-working drones, give them all grandiloquent titles —and then mire them down in bottomless quagmires of forms, reports, memoranda, "studies" and "surveys."

Thus, it is hardly surprising that so many young men start their business careers with the idea that "administration" is not only the tail that wags the whole business dog, but that it is, in itself, the whole animal. These young men will spend half their time trying to find out what they're doing through studies and surveys, then spend the other half informing each other about what—if anything—they've learned through the media of committee meetings and interoffice memoranda.

I'm still a wildcatter at heart, I suppose. I don't hold with the ultra-organization and superadministration theories at all. I still believe that the less overhead there is in business, the better. The world-wide complex of firms comprising the Getty interests manages to function beautifully with a modicum of administrative detail and paperwork. For example, there are only some 50 people doing administrative work in our entire Middle Eastern operation. The Getty Oil Company of Italy—which, in addition to its other operations, runs a 40,000-barrel-a-day refinery and a 1,300,000-barrel-capacity tank farm—has an administrative staff of only 15 persons. This proves—at least to my associates and me—that businesses *can* be operated successfully without proliferating paperwork empires. The thought may not please exponents of the "Everything in Quintuplicate" school, but the system certainly improves efficiency and boosts production. The resultant savings and increased profits make our stockholders very happy, indeed.

Yet another of the blunders of young businessmen and executives is their constantly increasing tendency to overspecialize. The young man who understands all aspects and phases of business is a rare bird these days. The average young executive has a thorough theoretical knowledge of one single facet of business but knows little or nothing about what goes on in any office or department save his own. He is like the mythical medical specialist who is so specialized that he only examines left nostrils.

If the trend continues, the real businessman—the man who can actually coordinate and run a business because he knows what makes it tick and how it operates—will disappear from the scene entirely. His place will no doubt be taken by some sort of supercybernetic machine. The machine will establish policy, make final decisions and give orders after bits and pieces of information encoded on punched tapes are fed into it by ultraspecialized company executives.

To succeed in a business, to reach the top, an individual must know all it is possible to know about that business. He must be acquainted with the duties and responsibilities of each and every section, office and department of the firm. He must know something—the more the better—about accounting as well as production, about sales as well as purchasing. Like the oldtime wildcatters, he should know a dozen—or a hundred—different jobs well enough so that he can exercise direct supervision, increase efficiency and product quality, reduce costs and still make a profit and continue to expand.

Any executive can do a much better job if he peels off his business suit once in a while, climbs into a set of overalls and gets his hands dirty down in the plant. The vice-president in charge of purchasing who has fed the raw materials he buys into a processing vat or a molding oven can do a much better job of purchasing. He can often learn more by listening to the conversation of a few production workers for an hour than he can by reading 10,000 specification sheets. Advertising and sales managers who have operated a lathe or punch press and have actually made a component of the product about which they rhapsodize will be much more convincing and successful in their sales campaigns. The employee-relations expert will have a much clearer and better understanding of employee problems and psychology if he spends more time among the employees and less in his paneled office dreaming up new "morale-building" gimmicks or bowling parties.

I don't suppose there are any finer examples to prove my point than the companies in the Bell Telephone System. There are few Bell System companies in which the top executives didn't work their way up through the ranks. They began as linemen, cable-splicers, bookkeepers. They generally moved around as well as up during their careers. They run their operations with remarkable efficiency.

Walter Munford, the late president of U.S. Steel, began his career as a die-reamer, working 78 hours per week—and came up the hard way. Harry B. Cunningham, president of S. S. Kresge, started as a stock boy and worked his way up through the various departments and levels of the giant retail chain. The list of such examples could be extended indefinitely, but the point, I think, is clear.

Another error that unseasoned businessmen make is that they relegate, rather than delegate, authority. I suppose it's natural for an executive or a man who owns a business to feel that he should take things as easily as possible. That's human nature—but it's hardly good business. A businessman can never afford to let down—nor can he afford to relegate his authority. If he allows others to run his business without maintaining close and constant supervision over their policies and operations, he's most likely to find that he has made a mistake and that he and his business are in trouble. All too often, by the time he makes that discovery, it's too late to do anything about it.

"If you have a business, make sure that you're the one who's running it," is a piece of advice I received many years ago. "If you don't want to accept the headaches of being boss, then either close the business down or sell it to someone who *will* accept the responsibilities." I've found this to be sound counsel. A businessman should delegate authority —he must, in fact, for no one man can be everywhere and do everything. But he must also remember that the final responsibility is his—and thus, he should always retain final authority.

This brings me to the last of the mistakes I've observed that young businessmen make frequently: their growing habit of pampering themselves—complaining that they're overworked and constantly laboring under "terrific strain and tension." They flaunt their real or imagined ailments— particularly their ulcers—as badges of honor. They spend huge amounts of time and money on medical checkups, cardiograms, X rays and tests and examinations of every conceivable kind. Nothing could be more nonsensical.

The National Office of Vital Statistics reveals that "men of the managerial, technical and administrative level as a whole have lower . . . than . . . average mortality rates." Business executives enjoy the lowest rates when buying life insurance. Medical studies indicate they are less susceptible to heart trouble—a favorite executive's bugaboo—than clerks or laborers, are no more inclined to contract cancer or most other fatal diseases than bricklayers or streetcar conductors.

"There's nothing really wrong with most executives," the head of a famous clinic once remarked to me. "They aren't overworked or overstrained. They're just overworried about holding their jobs and become nervous wrecks as a result of the office politics they so often play." Other doctors have told me they believe that many executives' morbid preoccupation with their health is a by-product of the status-seeking mania.

"Executives who are secretly afraid they aren't good enough to be promoted build up health alibis in advance," is the way one physician explained it. "In the event they fail to make good, they can convince their wives, their friends—and themselves—that their health, not their incompetence, was responsible for their failure."

One doctor even says that many executives who claim to have ulcers have nothing of the kind. "Having ulcers has become a status symbol," he grins. "There are certain types of executives who would rather die than admit they have nothing wrong with their stomachs. That would be tantamount to admitting that they were like the hoi polloi!"

Not being a medical authority, I can hardly pass judgment on any of these theories. I can, however, enjoy a hearty private laugh whenever I hear a 28- or 30-year-old executive who works at most 48 hours a week—less the time he spends having three-hour "business lunches" and playing golf—wail that he's "overworked" or "laboring under terrific strain." The truly great giants and geniuses of American business habitually worked 16- and 18-hour days—often seven days a week—and seldom took vacations. As a result, most of them lived to a ripe old age.

For example, Andrew Mellon was 82 when he died, Andrew Carnegie and Henry Ford lived to be 84, George L. Hartford and Samuel H. Kress died at 92. John D. Rockefeller, Sr., was 98 when he died.

Nor is this true only of businessmen of the past. Hugh Robertson was 72 in 1959 when he turned over the presidency of the Zenith Radio Corporation to Joseph S. Wright, and moved up to be a very active chairman of the board. Walter Johnson—in his eighties—is famous for the energy and ambition with which he runs two giant companies—Friden, Inc. and the American Forest Products Co. There are uncounted others like them.

The "half-strength" executive who complains about his "overwork" and its menace to his health would do well to buy a *Who's Who of American Businessmen* and study it carefully. He'd find that the hardest-working and most successful businessmen most often live longest.

These, then, are the various categories of blunders I've seen young businessmen make so frequently during my more than 40 years in the business world. Some are mistakes that a beginner will almost inevitably make until he is seasoned and matured in business. Others are errors that can be avoided, particularly if an individual is forewarned about them. Most of the blunders I've listed are errors I've committed myself at one time or another. In business or out of it, there's nothing unusual or shameful about making a mistake—once. But, as Cicero said, to stumble twice against the same stone is a proverbial disgrace.

THE PSYCHOLOGY OF
SOUND PERSONNEL
MANAGEMENT

No successful businessman has ever made his fortune without the dedicated help of his employees. The realization of almost every idea requires the intelligent work and cooperation of all involved. An ambitious executive must know how to summon the best from those around him, regardless of the pressure or lack of it. This is an essential skill that seems to come naturally to some, but can also be learned.

Many years ago, I had a conversation with one of America's leading industrialists, a man noted in business circles for operating his many companies with consistent success.

"You certainly seem to have a magic touch," I remarked at one point during our discussion.

"Magic touch?" the magnate said. "No, I don't think I have anything of the kind. The reason I've done pretty well is that I long ago discovered the secret ingredient that makes all the difference in business—the use in management of applied psychology based on common sense."

I could readily understand what he meant, for I had learned my first lessons about what sound psychology could do to make business management more efficient in the Oklahoma oil fields. I'll admit the lessons were blunt and basic—and sometimes even harsh—but then, this was to be expected when working with the men who formed my drilling crews.

I was young and relatively inexperienced; the men who worked for me were mostly older in years and much wiser in practical knowledge and experience. My position was somewhat analogous to that of a freshly commissioned second lieutenant who suddenly finds himself commanding a unit made up of tough, veteran regulars. I had the authority and the final responsibility; the seasoned campaigners watched with wary skepticism to see how I would use and discharge these, and waited for me to prove myself.

I knew it would be worse than useless for me to assume a stern, authoritarian role, to play the martinet; I would only appear ludicrous and reap nothing but contempt, which the men would show by doing as little work as possible. It would have been equally fatal for me to remain aloof or, on the other hand, to try to ingratiate myself by being overly familiar and pretending I was "one of the boys." I realized I would have to strike some viable median. I did not think of it as "psychology"; I doubt if I was then aware the term could even be used in any such context. It was simply a question of finding the most effective techniques for managing the activities of the men on whose morale and performance my business success hinged.

The direct approach seemed most advisable—if for no other reason than that the men would have instinctively sensed any attempt to "con" them. By one means and another, I made my views quite clear. I let the men see I respected them not only for their superior experience but also as individuals, and looked upon our association as a mutual effort in which I assumed the financial risks, accepted the major headaches and was willing to do my share of the work. I gave no orders or instructions without explanation, meticulously avoided meddling or nit-picking, but was always ready to lend a hand on even the messiest and most difficult tasks whenever a hand was needed.

Within a remarkably short time, my men were acknowledging that, although I was a tenderfoot, I was not a total ignoramus and, in fact, apparently possessed a fair amount of knowledge about the oil business in general and drilling operations in particular. We rapidly developed a strong degree of mutual respect, and work on the drilling site progressed quickly and efficiently. There were, of course, a few rough spots and potentially taut situations—one of which I particularly recall.

In those days, drilling crews worked twelve-hour shifts six days a week. This left little time for week-night sprees in town, but some of the men were unable to resist the temptations of the boomtowns, notwithstanding the fact that morning-after work in the broiling Oklahoma sun was brutal punishment. One morning, one of my roustabouts appeared on the drilling site suffering from a monumental hangover. Although we were at a crucial stage of drilling, he showed he had no intention of doing any serious work that day and began to openly soldier on the job.

The other members of the crew watched closely to see what—if anything—I would do. Luckily, two things were in my favor. I, myself, had been out the night before and the crew knew this, and the hung-over goldbricker was only a few years older than I was.

"Feeling rough?" I asked him. He just glowered at me. "I'll make you a deal," I went on. "I'll spot you ten seconds and race you up the rig. If you beat me, you can have the day off with pay."

The roustabout squinted up to the top of the drilling tower. "Boss, you're on," he grunted. I handed one of the other men my watch. At a signal, the roustabout started a monkey scramble up the rig. Exactly ten seconds later, I followed suit—and succeeded in reaching the crown block a second or two before him.

We were both winded when we got back down to the drilling platform—but it was obvious that I had won several victories. The other members of the crew were grinning broadly. I'd handled the situation in a manner that they could appreciate and had proved my right to be "boss." The roustabout was good-naturedly jeered—and he took it all in equally good stride.

"OK," he groaned. "I'll work this shift if it kills me!" He did work the shift—and it didn't kill him. Thereafter, he was one of the hardest-working and most conscientious members of the crew, and subsequently worked for me on many other drilling jobs.

I'll grant the incident is an elementary illustration of how applied psychology can solve management problems and help business operate more efficiently. I would hardly recommend that, say, the executive vice-president of a construction company enter into a hod-carrying competition with an apprentice bricklayer in order to prove his managerial bona fides. Nonetheless, the example serves to demonstrate that, in directing human activities, there is much to be said for employing methods and taking actions that have human appeal, that the individuals concerned can readily grasp.

I think my industrialist friend's definition of management might be stated in another way, namely that the primary function of management is to obtain results *through people*. Consequently, sound management psychology will motivate, direct, encourage and, in those exceptional instances where management is in the hands of exceptional individuals, inspire people so they will achieve the results that make possible the attainment of given objectives.

There was a time—happily, long past—when management gave little if any thought to the human material which has always formed the most valuable asset of any business. Employees were considered highly expendable, stockholders were at the mercy of manipulators and sharks, and attitudes toward even customers and clients found definitive expression in the classic utterance "The public be damned!"

The entire concept of management-people relations has undergone radical change in recent decades. Business and business management have grown up; they have become knowledgeable, sophisticated, aware that people count. Granted, the changes did not come about spontaneously; they were aided, even forced, by outside pressures. However, this is not of importance here. The important thing is that modern management has become acutely conscious that it must deal with and depend on human beings, that to get the most out of people it is necessary to do more than merely growl or shout an order and, above all, that human beings must be led and never driven.

Having recognized—and regretted—its past errors and oversights, the business community has done much to correct them and to develop an enlightened management psychology. Proof of this can be found in the extensive programs designed to maintain good employee, stockholder and public relations and in the effort most companies take to insure that they are "projecting a favorable corporate image." These are all significant manifestations of modern management's awareness that it can only obtain results through people.

Although, broadly speaking, all companies want to obtain very similar results—such as high employee morale, high levels of quality production, healthy profits—the patterns and methods of application of their management psychology vary not only in detail but also in effectiveness. Far too many executives at all levels still fail to comprehend that sound management psychology, like charity, begins at home and, while elaborate public-relations programs doubtless accomplish much, the place to start applying management psychology is no more distant than the nearest stenographer, machinist or salesclerk.

No psychological weapon is more potent than example. An executive who seeks to achieve results through the people who work under his direction must himself demonstrate at least as high a standard of performance as he hopes to get from his subordinates. If he makes a habit of spending three hours over lunch, he has no right to complain when his secretary dawdles an extra ten minutes over her coffee break or lacquers her nails when she should be typing a report the board chairman wants to see the next morning.

Executives need to establish and maintain single standards in other regards as well. Some fail to do so and exert a strong adverse psychological influence on their subordinates. There are those who adopt a *"quod licet jovi, non licet bovi"*—"what is permitted the gods is not permitted the cattle"—attitude, blandly assuming their rank not only bestows privileges but also grants license. Typical of the genus is the executive who issues menacing warnings about pilfering and the personal use of company-owned property. It's not beyond him to fire the office boy for appropriating a lead pencil or a five-cent stamp—yet this same man will blandly spend hours dictating personal letters to his secretary and will send subordinates out to run his personal errands on company time.

Workers are quick to learn of such things; a company grapevine is one of the swiftest means of communication known to our society. And, when an executive's bad example or his double standards become known, morale and output plummet in his department. I've encountered both types of men during the course of my career and can cite two representative examples from my experience when I was managing the Spartan Aircraft Company.

At one point, I became intuitively aware that employee

morale was sagging. I soon found out why. Several executives had gotten it into their heads they could arrive for work anywhere from 30 minutes to an hour late each morning. Naturally, this did not set very well with the rank-and-file workers who were required to punch time clocks and were docked pay if they were tardy.

Fire, it is said, can be best fought with fire—and I've always felt that bad management psychology is best countered by forcefully positive applied psychology. I did not waste time issuing threats of disciplinary action. I simply announced that, thenceforth and until further notice, I would hold daily conferences at which I expected all management personnel to be present—and the conference would begin promptly 45 minutes *before* the start of the regular working day.

I lost a bit of sleep in the next two weeks or so, but I won a major battle. My executives got the idea; there was no more habitual tardiness, and worker morale was restored to a high level in record time.

Not long thereafter, I learned an executive had taken some company-owned lumber and nails with which he constructed a dog kennel in his back yard. Although the lumber came from old, dismantled packing crates, I felt he'd set a dangerous precedent which could lead to all kinds of trouble and cause pilferage losses to soar if employees learned he'd gotten away with it. Since he was a valuable man, I did not want to fire him and relied on another applied-psychology stratagem to handle the situation. I sent the man a pleasantly worded memorandum, asking for a detailed inventory of the material he'd taken and saying I would have its appraised value charged against his salary. The inventory was prepared; the appraisal showed the total value to be about four dollars, and this sum was duly charged against his pay. I got the point across, not only to the executive concerned, but also to the thousands of Spartan employees, for the story made the rounds rapidly. We had remarkably little pilferage loss from then on. The workers, realizing that not even the "brass" could get away with appropriating company property, evidently took the lesson to heart themselves.

It should be obvious that the integrity of management personnel is a decisive factor in creating a sound management psychology that will work with subordinates, superiors, equals, customers and anyone else with whom executives or their company has contact. Executive integrity is a many-faceted thing. For example, the good executive who practices sound management psychology realizes he cannot bluff those with whom he deals, whether they be subordinates or superiors. Subordinates in particular can sense when the boss is bluffing, when he does not know the answer to a question or problem or has made a mistake and is trying to cover up. Nor should the executive resort to buck passing. Bluffing will only cause loss of respect, while a frank admission of error or ignorance will gain human respect. Buck passing will earn him nothing but the contempt of those who know he passed the buck and the mortal hatred of those to whom he passed it.

In dealing with employees, it is essential they be given recognition as human beings, as individuals. Nothing achieves this more effectively or establishes a healthier mental and emotional climate among workers than what has been termed "responsible participation."

Unquestionably, financial reward is the principal motivation that causes people to work. However, this is not the sole motivation. For the majority of people—even though they may not admit or even realize it—work satisfies a distinct psychological need. The need is most fully satisfied, and the worker is motivated to do his best, if he can feel, as Roger Falk puts it, "that he is participating responsibly, whether alone or in a group, in an enterprise the over-all objectives of which he can understand."

Yale's Professor E. W. Bakke states the proposition as a management responsibility to insure that an employee "understands the forces and factors at work in *his* world," in other words, in his own work environment. The employee who is told the whys and wherefores of the job he does, of the instructions that are given to him and the things that happen around him, is made to feel he is participating responsibly in the over-all operation, and is consequently a happier, more enthusiastic and better worker.

It is indeed sound management psychology to carry the process of making the worker feel he is participating responsibly several steps further. There is no more effective way of doing this than by letting the employee know his views are of interest to management. Where practicable, workers should be asked what they think of a problem, projected innovation or change. Not only will this produce a surprisingly large number of worth-while suggestions, but it will give the individual worker a sense of pride—a sense that he is participating, playing a significant role.

I have long been aware of the value—both intrinsic and morale-building—of consulting subordinates, asking their opinions and advice. More than a few times during my career, some grizzled driller, veteran machinist or alert secretary has hit upon simple solutions to problems that baffled me and my executives, or offered suggestions that proved of immense value.

It all adds up to this: The worker is not a brute animal or a robot that can only respond to command. Workers—at all levels—are thinking, feeling human beings. They derive psychological satisfaction from the knowledge that management is interested in their brains as well as their brawn and gives thought and consideration to their feelings.

Sound management psychology calls for continuing interest in all employee problems, even personal ones. This does not mean management should pry into any employee's private affairs. It does mean that management should lend a sympathetic ear—and, where reasonable, provide assistance—to an employee with personal problems.

This is done on a broad scale in many companies; there are employee-welfare programs, counseling services, credit bureaus and a host of similar facilities. Nonetheless, it is excellent psychology to carry this spirit through at all managerial levels. No, a department head should not be a father-confessor or a Dutch uncle to all his subordinates. On the other hand, if an executive is to achieve results through people, he must possess an element of compassion in his make-up, and must always bear in mind that every individual has his hopes, interests, problems and fears. If a worker respects his superior, it is human nature for him to seek the superior's counsel—and it is the soundest management psychology for the superior to hear him out and, if possible, help him.

Fairness is another major building block in the structure

of sound management psychology. Management must be fair to its employees, stockholders, customers and suppliers. Executives should not play favorites among their subordinates or customers. Stockholders are entitled to somewhat more than an even break. Suppliers cannot be treated capriciously. Salaries and wages paid to workers should be fair and equitable; promotions should be made on the basis of merit. The psychological impact of unfairness is likely to be shattering to the individual; failure to be fair at all times means just that for management: failure.

Among other things, fairness to employees implies trust. The feeling that he is not being trusted damages—and frequently destroys—employee morale and performance. No worker can be contented and productive if he senses that management distrusts his competence or distrusts him personally.

In his book *The Naked Society*, Vance Packard quotes Yale University's Dr. Chris Argyris, whose researches into human behavior have shown that "one of the most powerful motivators of constructive human conduct is simple trust." Packard goes on to cite what Dr. Argyris describes as a "causal chain" of mistrust that develops in some companies:

1. The employee comes into the organization with honest, earnest motives.

2. He experiences the frustration that comes from a feeling of failure because he is given little feeling that he is trusted and little responsibility.

3. He reacts by feeling less responsibility for the well-being and success of the organization. He also may gradually respond to his feeling of failure in a number of active ways, including stealing. Partly he steals because it is a safe way to express his aggression. In a deeper sense "he steals from a company which has helped to alienate him from feeling responsibility, commitment and trust."

4. Once the stealing occurs, management tightens up the very factors that caused the original stealings.

5. Now the distrust of the workers is out in the open. They begin to feel "OK, if they think I cannot be trusted, I will act as if I cannot."

Dr. Argyris has found in his studies that distrust is not confined to the lower-level employees. "In my opinion there is a lot of distrust at the upper levels," he states.

In discussing the psychology of sound management, one inevitably and invariably comes full circle, returning to the fact that business depends on people and cannot operate without them. It doesn't make much difference how much other knowledge or experience an executive possesses; if he is unable to achieve results *through people,* he is worthless as an executive.

LIVING
WITH
LABOR

Living with, working with labor—not fighting it or ignoring it—should be an assumed obligation of the business executive. Success and profits can be gained more easily—and happily—with labor's honest cooperation than without it. This should all be obvious, but deplorably few businessmen see labor relations as anything but an obstacle. Yet my own experiences have proven to me that a successful (and mutually respectful) liaison with labor *can* be achieved.

Some years ago, for example, representatives of a labor union sought to negotiate a new contract with a company I owned and I met with them at the bargaining table. Their demands centered around an hourly wage increase which I knew the company could not afford to grant in full. I did, however, believe we could meet the demands halfway and felt that such an increase was justified.

Before the negotiations began, my labor-relations "experts" urged me to give no hint of this in the early bargaining sessions. "Play it close to the vest," they advised. "Offer nothing at all until the last possible moment, when the talks reach an apparent impasse—as they doubtless will. Then start low and edge the offer up slowly, raising it only as much as is absolutely necessary."

To my way of thinking, this approach smacked strongly of bazaar haggling. It seemed to me that such a strategy was beneath the dignity of the company and an affront to the union representatives' intelligence and could only serve to cause lasting bitterness on both sides. As I owned the company outright and thus would not be taking risks with the interests of other stockholders, I had no compunctions about following my own, and in my opinion wiser, counsel. I decided to try an experiment.

I went to the initial bargaining session armed with a few simple—but accurate, informative—reports. These showed the company's production costs and output, its profit-and-loss statement for the previous year, and reviewed its over-all financial situation and the outlook for the immediate future. I listened patiently while labor stated its position and demands. Then I handed the documents I'd brought with me to the union spokesman and took the floor.

"I suppose we could be here for days, arguing back and forth," I said. "But, as far as I'm concerned, it's more sensible to start off where we'd have to end up in any case. The company is unable to give you all you're asking—the reports I just handed you will prove that. You *can* have half the wage boost—and that's the absolute limit at the present time. If production and profits rise in the next year, I'll be glad to talk seriously with you about the other half."

Having said my piece, I glanced around the table, noting with considerable amusement that my aides looked horrified, and the union representatives appeared astounded. I thereupon suggested a recess—a suggestion the labor side seized upon gratefully. We adjourned the meeting, agreeing to resume it in the late afternoon.

My assistants were glum. They were certain I had taken the first steps toward giving away not only my company, but my shirt and theirs as well. They were convinced I'd handed the union the proverbial inch—and that it would consequently insist on taking its mile. At best, they expected the union to double its demands; at worst, they feared a long, costly strike.

When the meeting resumed, my aides filed into the conference room with the air of men being led to the tumbrels. I said nothing, but grinned inwardly at their discomfiture. I still believed I had assessed the situation correctly and had followed the right course, a belief soon verified by the union spokesman's opening remarks.

"To tell you the truth, we thought we were in for a long, tough fight," he declared. "But you laid everything on the line and gave us all the facts at the beginning—so there's really nothing to argue about." He paused and reached across the table to shake my hand.

"Mr. Getty, you've just gotten yourself a new contract," he announced with a broad smile. The remaining details were quickly agreed upon and the contract duly signed. My "experiment" proved to be a success that had long-lasting and beneficial aftereffects.

Within the next 12 months, production and profits rose sufficiently to justify granting an additional wage increase. A lasting bond of mutual respect was established between management and labor. To this day, any disputes are still discussed and settled in the same sort of atmosphere, and the company has been singularly free of labor strife. The straightforward approach backed by facts worked—just as it has in most similar situations I've encountered during my years as a businessman and employer.

The incident is illustrative of my over-all experience, in that I've usually found that organized labor is fundamentally fair—but that it wants to know the facts. And, when I say facts, I mean precisely that. I do *not* mean tailored versions, half-truths or vague platitudes.

Workers and union officials are not ignoramuses. They are perfectly capable of recognizing attempts to mislead or misinform them—and, like anyone else, they are quite likely to resent and rebel against such treatment. On the other hand, once they are given the unvarnished facts, the representatives of honest labor unions are generally cooperative to the maximum extent consistent with their legitimate aims and their responsibilities toward their members.

I have not encountered any very great amount of trouble with labor during my business career. Possibly this is due in some degree to my own attitude toward labor. Unlike some businessmen, I've never objected to the activities of free, honest labor unions. I recognize the right of labor to organize and bargain with management, because I recognize the innate human urge to a better life. Being a realist, I understand that for many—possibly most—people, this urge translates into a desire to have the best possible working conditions and the highest possible living standards, and manifests itself in the traditional demands for shorter hours and more pay.

True, there are limits—set by such factors as production and profits—beyond which it is impossible for management to reduce hours and increase wages. It is management's responsibility to convince labor of this, to define the limits clearly and furnish irrefutable facts to prove its case. I'll agree that in this sense, management does have to engage in give-and-take skirmishing with organized labor—but this is a matter of reasoned argument, not class war.

I certainly have no patience with the all-too-familiar variety of organization man who habitually and indiscriminately denounces organized labor. I've frequently observed that most vociferous union haters of this type are individuals who demand for themselves identically the same advantages they condemn organized labor for seeking.

For example, interviews conducted recently with young executives and business students show that the majority declares itself to be against unions. At the same time, some 75 percent of them cite security as the principal reason why they work—or want to work—for large corporations:

"There's very little chance of getting fired or laid off . . ."

"Regular salary increases . . ."

"Retirement and medical benefits . . ."

"Yearly vacations with pay . . ."

Now, I would begrudge no executive what so many of them have evidently come to regard as their due—be it job tenure or an annual holiday. But I see no logic or consistency in the admittedly security-seeking organization man's opposition to organized labor's search for a similar degree of security.

Like it or not, labor unions are here to stay—and so are the benefits they have won for their members. The days when a laborer earned a dollar for 12 hours' work and Henry Ward Beecher could publicly thunder that a worker who was not content to live on bread and water was "not fit to live" are gone.

None but the most antediluvian specimens dwelling in the murky fens of reaction's lunatic fringe would want to turn the clock back to the sweatshop era. Enlightened modern-day business understands and accepts the need for trade unions, which labor historian Frank Tannenbaum has called "visible evidence that man is not a commodity, and that he is not sufficient unto himself."

Calumet & Hecla executive H. Y. Bassett expressed the modern business view in his frequently quoted essay, *What Does Industry Expect of a Community?* "Progressive managements have no quarrel with unions, but on the contrary feel that they have a place in the present-day world of business," Bassett declared.

The late Charles E. ("Engine Charlie") Wilson's comments on annual-improvement and cost-of-living pay increases reflect progressive businessmen's attitudes toward the security benefits gained by labor unions in recent years. "What we are doing is exploiting machines, not men," Wilson said. "It is logical, fair and reasonable to maintain the purchasing power of an hour's work in terms of goods and services the employee must purchase." He was clearly aware of a basic economic truth which lesser businessmen unaccountably often choose to ignore or overlook—namely, that the worker is no longer just a worker. He is also a consumer—a customer.

The entire complex operational framework of modern business rests on the foundations of mass production. And, where there is mass production, there must also be mass consumption—mass markets. Otherwise, there are insufficient outlets for the production, the pace of business slows and the economy withers.

Today, labor forms a sizable segment of the mass markets which consume and use the goods and services mass-produced by business. Labor's prosperity—its high earnings and consequent high buying power—represents an important factor in the prosperity of the nation as a whole. Free and honest—and I strongly emphasize the words free and honest—labor unions have helped raise the living standards not only of the American worker, but of every American citizen. The gains organized labor has won at the bargaining table have, by raising the workers' buying power, contributed materially to the country's growth. The myth that labor is out to wreck the free-enterprise system has been lovingly nurtured in certain quarters. I, for one, could not disagree more. I cannot see that free, honest American unions pose any threat to American capitalism. If anything, they are among democracy's strongest bulwarks against political or economic totalitarianism.

I've observed that most American workers are well aware that they are enjoying benefits and a living standard they could never find in any other country or under any other political or economic system. The majority of U.S. labor leaders are cognizant of the grim alternatives to the free-enterprise system and they have no taste for them, be they alternatives offered by the extreme left or right.

The fact that our economy is thriving—that our gross national product now exceeds *half a trillion dollars annually* —would seem sufficient to refute any charge that labor is wrecking or seeking to wreck that economy. Even more convincing proof is provided by yet another fact often ignored or conveniently forgotten by chronic union haters: our free-enterprise economy has burgeoned during the very period that labor unions gained their greatest strength.

"Our members may clamor for higher wages, shorter hours and fringe benefits," a prominent labor leader told me. "But neither they nor union officials want to destroy or even change the American free-enterprise system. Labor knows it has a big stake in business—but it wants business to realize that it, in turn, has an equally big stake in labor."

This is reasonable enough—and so are what my experience as a businessman and employer have shown me to be labor's two basic aims. First of all, labor wants to share in the wealth it helps create. Second, it wants recognition of its importance—not from the standpoint of the trouble it can cause, but rather from the standpoint that it does, after all, do the actual work of producing the goods and providing the services which business sells.

There is nothing unreasonable about the first aim—provided labor understands that wages and other rewards and benefits constituting its share of the wealth *must* be keyed to production and profits. This, unfortunately, is an axiom many workers—and even some labor leaders—sometimes fail to grasp. Management must explain this axiom and drive home its implications at every opportunity in all its dealings with labor. No effort should be spared to acquaint every employee with the fundamental truth of business arithmetic —that, in order to survive, a company has to earn more money than it spends. Labor must be made to understand that it is necessary for production rates to be maintained or even increased and a reasonable profit earned before wage increases can be contemplated. I have found that this can be done successfully in most instances, provided management can substantiate its statements.

There really aren't many legitimate labor leaders who have any desire to wreck a company that has a contract with their union. Most will even cooperate in finding ways to increase production if they are convinced it's necessary to keep the company solvent or if it will mean better pay or greater security for the members of their union. In such cases, it's up to management to do the convincing—with facts. It all adds up to one thing: Working together, instead of fighting each other, both capital and labor can achieve their material aims—each can share in the wealth their combined efforts create.

Helping labor realize its second aim is no less important. To satisfy labor's desire for recognition, management must give it just that. Management must show that it appreciates the importance of the individuals who actually perform the work. The responsibility and capacity for accomplishing this rests, largely, with the individual executive who, to the worker, represents and even personifies management.

I never cease to be amazed by the numbers of executives who do not realize the value of personal contact with rank-and-file employees. In some companies, the only times a production worker is likely to see a high-level executive are during full-dress Army-style inspection tours or when company "brass" escort VIP visitors through the plant.

Oh, yes. Then there are the executive visits occasionally staged by the company's public-relations department. The scenario for such an expedition usually follows a routine something like this: At a given hour—generally in the late morning or midafternoon—an impeccably dressed vice-president and a covey of bustling retainers descend on the plant. The party hesitantly and cautiously picks its way along the aisles between the rows of unfamiliar, noisy machines and stops, say, in front of a lathe. The vice-president fidgets, adjusts his necktie, shoots his cuffs and self-consciously edges closer to the lathe. He tries to look interested in the work being done on the machine and pretends to talk to the lathe operator—whose name has just been whispered into his ear, and which he has garbled.

Two or three photographers raise their cameras and focus on the dismal tableau. Flash bulbs flare, the vice-president mumbles something unintelligible—and he and his retinue beat a hasty retreat, returning to the pine-paneled peace and quiet of the company's downtown administrative offices.

A photograph of the vice-president and the lathe operator appears in the local paper the next day—and in the company's house organ the following week. "Mr. Wilbur Knowall, Bollix and Company's vice-president in charge of personnel, maintains close contact with the firm's employees," the caption under the picture reads. "He is shown conducting one of his frequent on-the-job interviews with Joe Smith, a lathe operator who has been with Bollix and Company for nearly three years."

The comments of Joe Smith and his fellow production workers when they see this are best left to the imagination. The only ones fooled by the transparent stunt are Mr. Wilbur Knowall and the company's so-called public-relations director.

Self-respecting workers resent such stunts which make a mockery of what has been called the dignity of labor—and so would I, if I were an employee of a "Bollix and Company." But then, my attitudes about work and toward labor were formed in the oil fields, where the inflexible governing rule was: The man who works for you is entitled to decent wages, decent working conditions—and your respect.

My years in those oil fields taught me that the men who actually *do* the work are most certainly entitled to decent wages and working conditions and their employers' respect. I also learned that nothing inspires worker loyalty or builds worker morale more swiftly than an employer's recognition of his employees' importance and his sincere interest in their well-being.

"A man likes to feel what he's doing is important—and that the boss looks at him as a person, not just a number on the payroll," is the way a veteran driller once expressed it to me. "A man always does better if he figures he's actually part of the operation, not just a hired hand working on the job—and it sure makes him feel good if the boss comes around now and then to see how he's making out."

Executives who stay awake nights trying to find better ways to improve employee loyalty, morale and efficiency would do well to paste this old-time driller's words into their Homburgs. They could spend years searching for a better answer or more reliable formula. Cheap stunts and tinselly morale-building schemes are definitely *not* the answer. The average worker is quick to see through the bogus stratagems inept or inexperienced management personnel are likely to devise.

The important thing is to let the worker know that he and his work *are* important to the company—and to believe it and mean it. Any executive who doesn't believe the rank-and-file employees are really important has no right to be an executive, for he obviously doesn't have a sense of proportion or know what makes business tick.

As a matter of fact, it's not difficult to imagine situations in which the hourly-wage employee is far more important than the salaried executive. Thomas Jones may have the exalted title of third assistant vice-president, and he may—and probably does—consider himself indispensable. But my guess would be that he's far more expendable than, say, a crack punch-press operator on the assembly line. Were Jones to vanish suddenly from the scene, his secretary—and he's sure to have at least one—can probably run things until he returns or until a replacement is found for him. In any event, the company will keep on going without Jones. But the absence of the punch-press operator might well slow or even halt a production line—and, in the last analysis, it's the production line and the products which come off it that count most.

The executive who understands and assumes his responsibilities takes every legitimate opportunity to demonstrate to his subordinates that he considers their work important and valuable—and that he respects them as workers and as individuals. And he takes a sincere interest in their well-being. He does not flatter, patronize or coddle them. He does, however, always manage to find time to comment on a particular job that has been especially well done or to acknowledge the value of a worker's or an entire department's contribution to the success of a project. In short, he shows by word and action that he and the company are aware of the workers' existence and of the importance of their work. By so doing, he goes a very long way toward raising employee morale—and when morale rises, employee efficiency and production go up while such profit-devouring headaches as absenteeism and labor turnover go down.

The good executive does not disdain checking personally on working conditions and takes prompt remedial action when he finds them below standard. A broken rest-room washbasin may seem a minor thing. But, if the executive— as a representative of management—gets it repaired before the shop steward can bring the matter up before the grievance committee, the executive will be taking a major step toward building good labor-management relations.

Believe me, the remedies for many labor-management problems are just about that simple. When the desires and demands of labor are boiled down to their essentials and viewed objectively, they no longer loom as the deadly business-destroying menaces they are often represented to be. They shrink and become entirely understandable—and there is nothing unnatural, immoral or subversive about them. Labor's basic desires and demands are succinctly stated in that oil-fields adage—the right to decent wages, decent working conditions—and respect.

Management executives accepting this tried and proven rule and governing themselves by it are able to live with labor comfortably, successfully—and profitably. As any successful businessman will tell you, learning to live with labor is sound business.

THE
BUSINESSMAN
AT BAY

Crises, setbacks, obstacles—these will certainly be met by any executive in the course of his career. The measure of a man in such circumstances is not only how he copes with adversity, but also how he turns it to his advantage. Business is always a battle—for sales, improvements, efficiency —and an executive must lead very much as a general would: to win.

I remember learning as a youth an invaluable lesson from a man who even then had extensive business holdings and who later became one of America's wealthiest industrialists. Although I knew him fairly well, I hadn't seen him for several months before bumping into him one day in the lobby of a Chicago hotel.

"How are things going?" I asked him after we'd exchanged the customary greetings.

"Not good—terrible, in fact," he replied with a placid smile. "One of my companies has been shoved into a tight corner by the competition. Another is operating in the red —and a third hasn't the cash to meet its short-term debts that fall due this month."

"You certainly don't act as though any of it worries you very much," I remarked in surprise. I found it hard to believe that any businessman who was in so much apparent trouble could be so casual about his problems.

"Hell, Paul, I'm not in the least bit worried," he answered. "To tell you the truth, I needed something like this to get me up on my toes; everything had been going entirely too smoothly for far too long. An occasional crisis is good for a businessman. There's no better exercise for him than to have a few messes to clean up every now and then."

Later, I learned that it had taken my friend less than six months to clean up all his "messes." Despite the fact that he owned or controlled many other business enterprises, he plunged enthusiastically into the task of personally reorganizing and revitalizing the three faltering companies.

He quickly pulled the first one out of the corner into which it had been driven by its competitors. He began improving old products, developing new ones and launching an imaginative, aggressive sales campaign that turned the tables on competing firms. He then put the second firm back on its feet by initiating new policies and programs, reducing production costs and increasing output. As for the third company, he arranged refinancing of its obligations, made needed changes in management personnel and soon had the firm on a sound financial footing and operating at a comfortable profit.

"I had quite a workout getting things in order," he told me sometime later. "But I sure enjoyed it—it's always more fun to win a hard fight than an easy one."

"Adversity is the first path to truth," Lord Byron said more than a hundred years ago.

"Calamity is man's true touchstone," Francis Beaumont and John Fletcher wrote in the early 17th Century.

Now, Byron and Beaumont and Fletcher were not businessmen and they did not concern themselves with business in their writings. Yet, the basic truths implicit in their lines are applicable to every present-day businessman and to anyone who hopes to make a success of a business career.

A machine that is functioning perfectly needs only nominal care. By the same token, a highly prosperous business that operates year after year without problems requires little more than caretaker management. No exceptional ability is needed to run such an enterprise. Unfortunately, the "perfect business" does not exist. Snags, difficulties and crises crop up in every business. For the businessman—as for any individual—the true test of his mettle comes at the time when he is faced with adversity.

How do executives or businessmen act and react when they are at bay?

First, there are those who sit by helplessly, allowing whatever adversity they face to overwhelm them completely.

They are like rabbits which, transfixed by the headlights of an automobile rushing toward them on a highway, make no move to save themselves and are consequently crushed under the vehicle's wheels. Such men take no action to change the course of events and prevent disaster because they are incapable of comprehending what could or might be done. When they have been finally overwhelmed, they are stunned, totally unable to understand what went wrong and why.

Then, there are those who surrender meekly or flee in fear as soon as things start to go wrong. Such men have little or no sense of proportion; they are likely to panic and view even minor slumps and setbacks as unavoidable major catastrophes. While individuals in the first category fail to fight back because they do not know how to fight, businessmen who can be classed in this second group fail to fight back because they are afraid to do so.

Next come those men who react to adversity in an unreasonable, almost hysterical fashion. Terror-stricken, they snarl and snap, striking back blindly and ineffectually, squandering their energies in the wrong directions. These men invariably rail and curse against the "impossible odds" and "rotten breaks" they claim defeated them. Just as invariably, they seek to lay the blame for the predicaments in which they find themselves on shoulders other than their own.

In another category are those businessmen who fight good, tenacious—and, very frequently, entirely successful —defensive actions whenever things start to go wrong. They are courageous, reliable individuals who unflinchingly meet threats and solve problems as they arise, acting to the best of their not-inconsiderable abilities. But there they stop. Their minds are geared to thinking solely in terms of plugging the holes in the dike as, if and when they appear. The men in this group do not have the imagination and initiative— or lack the experience—to think and plan in terms of building entirely new and much stronger dikes in which holes will be far less likely to develop.

Finally, there are those businessmen who are the real leaders. These are the imaginative, aggressive individuals who base their business philosophy on the ancient military axiom that attack—or, at the very least, energetic counterattack—is invariably the best defense. Obviously, they can't—and don't—always win, but then no general in the world's history has ever won *every* battle he fought.

On the other hand—to carry the analogy between business affairs and military campaigns a bit further—the generals who win the wars and have the highest percentage of victories to their credit are those who can mastermind defensive strategy as well as an offense.

The truly great general views reverses calmly and coolly; he is fully aware that they are bound to occur occasionally and refuses to be unnerved by them. When driven back, he prevents retreat from turning into rout and then adroitly transforms the retreat into an orderly retrograde movement.

By so doing, he disengages his forces from those of the enemy with a minimum of additional loss, saving the bulk of his manpower and material resources so that they can be regrouped and made ready for a counterattack. Naturally, he leaves behind rear guards to protect the withdrawal. He accepts the losses these covering forces must inevitably suffer with philosophical stoicism, realizing that it is sometimes necessary to sacrifice a part in order to save the whole.

When his troops have been rested and reinforced and his supplies replenished, the successful general launches his carefully planned counterattack. Having studied the situation with great care and having learned much about the enemy's capabilities and habits from an analysis of what has gone before, he employs a combination of every resource at his command. He makes feinting and diversionary assaults, aims his major blows at the weakest points in the enemy line and holds back his reserves until he can commit them at the right—at the decisive—times and places.

Like the successful military leader, the successful, veteran businessman understands that he cannot master every business situation, that he cannot emerge victorious from every business "battle." He knows that, sooner or later, he will encounter problems which cannot be solved quickly or easily, that he will find his progress blocked by obstacles which will require much time and effort to overcome or which will even force him to retrace his steps and take a new route. He knows that reverses and losses are sometimes inevitable.

The seasoned business campaigner is well aware that the line charting the course of any company's history or any businessman's career on a graph would be a jagged one. The graph would reflect a series of alternating peaks and lows. But such ups and downs do not bother the seasoned businessman unduly. He recognizes that the significant and telling proof lies in whether the line at the right edge of the chart terminates at a point that is higher or lower than the point at which it begins on the left.

True business leaders—the real *leaders*—often give their most impressive demonstrations of leadership and brilliance at the very times when they are temporarily forced to go over to the defensive, at the times when they are at bay. And this is precisely what sets them apart and raises them above the level of other, less successful businessmen.

Take, for example, the case of my friend who found himself in three serious business predicaments simultaneously. There were several courses of action this businessman might have followed. He could have done nothing, allowing matters to take their own course. He could have closed or sold one or more of the companies, utilizing whatever money he realized from any sale or sales to shore up whatever remained. He might have been content merely to plug the holes.

But he neither surrendered nor panicked. Nor was he satisfied with doing a hasty job. A good general, he surveyed the situation thoroughly, reorganized his forces, brought up replacements and reinforcements and made his plans. Then, marshaling all his resources, he launched successful counterattacks on all three fronts.

The history of American business and industry is replete with examples of how the great business leaders of the nation handily turned serious reverses into major triumphs.

It was in 1903 that Henry Ford began manufacturing automobiles of his own. In 1908, he produced the first famous Model T and soon captured a very large share of the burgeoning U. S. automobile market.

Ford continued to mass-produce the Model T until 1927, making few drastic changes in the comparatively primitive model during that entire time. But, by 1926, Chevrolet—Ford's biggest and most dangerous competitor in the low-priced field—was turning out more powerful, comfortable and stylish cars. Ford still used the foot-pedal-controlled, planetary transmission; Chevrolet had a geared transmission. Chevrolet was producing models in attractive colors; the Model T was still available only in black.

The automobile-buying public had grown more sophisticated. It wanted more speed, comfort and style. Ford rapidly began to lose ground to Chevrolet. Ford sales fell off alarmingly, while "Chevy" sales skyrocketed. The trend was well-defined—and many experts predicted that it was irreversible. They prophesied that Ford would never be able to catch up again; the company was well on the downhill road to becoming just another of the scores of automobile-manufacturing firms that had enjoyed a period of success only to fail subsequently.

These experts failed to estimate the aggressive genius of Henry Ford correctly. He was losing ground to the competition. He was at bay. But he was far from defeated—and even further from admitting defeat.

In the spring of 1927, Henry Ford shut down his enormous factory. Although it had been announced that he would bring out a new model, there were many rumors that the Ford plant would never reopen, or that when it did, the new Ford would be a dud, nothing more than just another obsolescent Model T with a superficial face lifting.

Then, in December 1927, the Ford Motor Company introduced its Model A to the market. Henry Ford marshaled all his forces—engineering, styling, production and sales—and launched a counterattack that memorably pulverized all competition.

A somewhat similar and more recent example in the automotive industry was provided by American Motors and its then head, energetic George Romney. Faced with falling sales and mounting losses, American Motors and Romney staged a spectacular comeback with their Rambler models.

In 1952, the Chicago meat-packing firm of Wilson & Co. lost $763,000. James D. Cooney became the company's president the following year and, according to some of his associates, "turned the company inside out and around so that it was pointed in the right direction." Wilson & Co.'s 1959 earnings exceeded $9,500,000.

In 1933, the outlook for banks and bankers was bleak, indeed. The Depression had reached its lowest point. The Federal Government had ordered the memorable "Bank Holiday" on March 6th of that year. More than 4000 banks throughout the country failed, suspended operations or were placed in receivership during 1933.

One banker who ignored the widespread cries of impending calamity and went ahead to build his banking business was Walter Bimson of Arizona's Valley National Bank. Instead of running for cover and tightening up on loan policy, Bimson went out to "sell" loans to Arizonans in need of money. That his imagination and aggressive, courageous policies paid off is proven by the fact that though, in 1933, Valley National had deposits of less than $8,000,000, today, the Arizona bank can boast that deposits have swollen phenomenally to over $765,000,000.

In 1959, Thomas E. Sunderland moved out of the oil business—and into the fruit business. He took over the presidency of the giant United Fruit Company, accepting a job that many lesser men would have feared—or even refused to touch. The outlook for the future at United Fruit was hardly a glowing one when he stepped into the top executive position. Eight years earlier, in 1951, the company had made a profit of more than $50,000,000. In the years that followed, profits skidded—dropping to $12,000,000 in 1959 and dipping even lower to less than $3,000,000 in 1960.

Thomas Sunderland soon proved that he deserves to be ranked high among the elite of the business world. Sunderland gave the huge company a thorough, top-to-bottom overhaul. Confident and enthusiastic, he launched a massive counterattack against all the factors which were causing United Fruit's profits to fade. He shifted personnel, revised policy, modernized methods, reduced costs and increased efficiency. He achieved remarkable results in record time. In 1961, United Fruit reported that second-quarter profits alone exceeded $6,500,000. The company's stock, which had slumped as low as 17¼, had risen to 27⅜ by January 1962.

Anyone having knowledge of the American business scene could cite countless other examples paralleling these random few that I have mentioned. All would further help to prove that when the really topflight businessman is at bay, he very often turns adversity and even impending calamity into victory.

I've encountered my share of adversity and reverses. I've spent fortunes drilling many thousands of feet into the ground at one time or another—to strike nothing but sand. I've had other wells that cost other fortunes run dry or blow up and burn. I soon learned to accept such misfortunes philosophically and to take them in my stride, for I realized that I would not be able to stay in business very long if I permitted them to discourage me. In fact, each setback seemed to serve as a special incentive and stimulus to try again—but even harder the next time.

There were many other, more complex trials and blows, too. I recall, for example, the sharp break in crude-oil prices that occurred in 1921, when oil, which had been selling at $3.50 per barrel, dropped to $1.75 per barrel in less than 10 days—and the price continued to spiral down in the days that followed. At least one of the companies in which I held a substantial interest became hard-pressed for cash as a result of the price crisis.

When I met with other directors of the company, there were those among them who verged on panic. Fortunately, the majority remained calm and objective. Any suggestions that the company close its doors were immediately voted down. Instead, it was agreed to retrench and the directors agreed to obtain the money needed to keep the company going. They also agreed to slash their compensation to the bone and reduce management salaries until the crisis was past. In time, the petroleum market became stabilized once more—and as soon as conditions returned to normal, the directors and management implemented an ambitious program which greatly increased the company's sales and profits within a very short period.

I also have vivid recollections of a memorable campaign my associates and I conducted to obtain control of a large company. The incumbent—and well-entrenched—directors of the company fought us fiercely at every step. However, although the financial resources at our disposal were far less than those of the opposition, we managed to do a bit more than merely hold our own and the battle seesawed for a considerable time.

Then, at one point, the opposition sensed that I had almost exhausted my financial resources by buying the company's stock—and that for a time I would be unable to purchase any more. As I was still far short of having a controlling interest in the company, the incumbent directors believed that they now had the upper hand. Swiftly changing their tactics, they decided to allow the issue to be decided by all the stockholders.

This, of course, meant a proxy contest. In a burst of chivalrous magnanimity, the opposition entered into a sort of "gentleman's agreement" with our side. To prevent the proxy contest from degenerating into a rough-and-tumble fight that could injure the company's reputation, solicitation of proxies would be limited to one reasonably worded letter from each side. The two letters—one urging the stockholders to give their proxies to the incumbent board—would be mailed in the same envelope to each stockholder. Thus, the individual stockholder would have both sides of the story before him—and he could make his own decision as to which of the two groups best deserved to control the company.

My associates and I unhesitatingly accepted what we considered to be a gentlemanly agreement. Our letter was duly composed, reproduced and sent off together with the one prepared by the opposition. When that had been done, I assumed that the die was cast and that nothing further would be—or could be—done to influence the outcome.

Then, only a few days before the scheduled stockholders' meeting, one of my aides burst into my office. His face was livid with anger and he clutched a piece of paper in his hand.

"Read this!" he exclaimed, thrusting the paper at me. I took it and found that it was a letter—a *second* letter—which the opposition had sent out to the stockholders only a day or two earlier. And what a letter it was!

The gist of the no-holds-barred missive was a virulent personal attack on me and a highly objectionable—and entirely baseless—implication that my motives for seeking control of the company were, at best, dubious. I called my associates and held a hasty council of war. What could be done at that late stage of the game? Not much, some of my associates declared dispiritedly. There wasn't enough time.

"I'm afraid this licks us, Paul," one man said, shaking his head in resignation. "Nothing in this letter is true—but it's going to have a tremendous impact on the stockholders. Not having any way of checking up on the charges that have been made, they'll play it safe and give their proxies to the other side."

"You really think we're licked?" I asked, glancing around at the men in the room with me. Some heads nodded assent. The faces of some other men showed that they weren't entirely convinced that all was lost. A few of my associates indicated that they refused to accept defeat that easily.

"Nuts!" one of them snorted. "We still have a chance!"

"I think so, too," I said. "Now, let's get to work."

Working feverishly against a deadline that was far too close for comfort, we composed our own second letter. Instead of calumny, we stated facts and figures that demolished every argument and charge advanced by the opposition.

Then, working straight through the day and night and the day that followed, we—secretaries, clerks, typists, executives, my associates and I—reproduced the letters, addressed envelopes to thousands of stockholders, folded and inserted the letters and sealed and stamped the envelopes. At last, we finished the staggering job—and exhausted men and women carried bundles of the letters to the nearest post office for mailing.

Would the letters reach the stockholders in time? We could only hope, and wait to see what happened at the stockholders' meeting a few days later. But we didn't have to wait that long. The response to our second letter was astounding. Replies began to pour in from stockholders two days before the meeting.

"We might make it yet," one of my aides remarked. And we did make it. Cold facts, stated clearly and plainly, proved to be more convincing to the stockholders than were the heated, personal attacks and irresponsible charges that had been made by the opposition. To the shocked amazement of the incumbent directors—and the delight of my associates and myself—the voting at the stockholders' meeting resulted in a clear-cut victory for our side!

Just a few years ago, it appeared that I was facing another serious—and potentially catastrophic—impasse. Exploration and drilling operations conducted by a company in which I held a very large interest indicated that the Middle Eastern areas in which it held drilling concessions would soon be producing crude oil in fantastic quantities. Unfortunately, various factors and restrictions would prevent importing more than a fraction of the production into the United States.

On the face of things, the outlook was anything but bright. Before long, immense quantities of crude oil would be pouring up out of the ground—but unless something was done, and quickly, most of it would be virtually worthless. Crude oil is, after all, only a raw material. It must be refined into other products which must then be distributed and marketed.

As time went on and more and more wells came in, there were those who openly predicted that I would soon find myself in a position from which I could not extricate myself. After spending staggering sums on obtaining the concession and on exploration and drilling, the company would be left with oceans of crude oil which it could not market. There were even those who gleefully rumored that it wouldn't be long before Paul Getty would be in serious financial trouble.

I'll admit the corner was getting a bit uncomfortable—but it was far from being so tight that there was no way out of it. To the chagrin of those who were predicting that the Getty interests would soon drown in their oceans of excess crude oil, we found—in fact, we virtually created—new outlets for our production. If we couldn't ship all our crude to the United States for refining and sale, we would ship it elsewhere, even if we had to buy or build our own refineries in other countries. And that is precisely what we did, buying one almost brand-new refinery in Italy, building another one in Denmark and finding other refinery capacity elsewhere. Now, of course, the Getty interests are avidly searching for *more* crude oil in the Middle East and elsewhere in the world.

Experiences such as these—and there have been many of them—have taught me that the time for the businessman to think and fight hardest is when the tide seems to be running against him and his prospects appear bleak. He can frequently turn even the worst of bad business situations to the advantage of his company, his stockholders and himself.

The Businessman at Bay

The successful businessman—the true business leader—is the individual who develops the ability to retain his composure in times of stress and in the face of setbacks. The young businessman should strive to acquire and develop this and the related traits I have previously mentioned—and he should try very early in his career, for it will not be long before he encounters his first reverses and adversities. The manner in which he meets the first few tight situations in which he finds himself will often set the pattern for the rest of his career.

Plainly, it is not possible for anyone to give a businessman specific, step-by-step advice on what he should—or should not—do when he suffers business reverses. There are far too many variables; each situation differs greatly from the next. On the other hand, there are certain fundamental principles which will greatly aid any businessman in meeting adverse situations and transforming setbacks into successes:

1. No matter what happens, do not panic. The panic-stricken individual cannot think or act effectively. A certain amount of trouble is inevitable in any business career—when it comes, it should be met with calm determination.

2. When things go wrong, it is always a wise idea to pull back temporarily—to withdraw just long enough and far enough to view and evaluate the situation objectively.

3. In the opening stages of any developing adverse situation, it may be necessary and advisable to give some ground, to sacrifice those things which are least important and most expendable. But it should be a fighting withdrawal, a retrograde action that goes back only so far and no further. It must never be a disorderly retreat.

4. Next, all factors in the situation must be examined with meticulous care. Every possible course of action must be weighed. All available resources—cerebral as well as financial, creative as well as practical—must be marshaled.

5. Countermoves must be planned with the greatest care and in the greatest of detail—yet with allowances for alternative courses in the event unforeseen obstacles are encountered. Counteraction must be planned on a scale consistent with the resources available—and the goals set must be conceivably attainable. It is well to bear in mind, however, that the impetus of a properly executed counterattack very often

carries the counterattacking force far beyond the point from which it was driven in the first place.

6. Once everything is ready, action should be taken confidently, purposefully, aggressively—and above all, enthusiastically. There can be no hesitation—and it is here that the determination, personality and energy of the leader count the most.

The businessman—young or old—who guides himself according to these principles when he has suffered reverses will not remain at bay very long.

THE
IMP OF
THE IMPOSSIBLE

Good judgment and imaginative foresight are two qualities which, working together, *can* make the "impossible" possible. The valuable habits of healthy skepticism and individual confidence can, and often do, help a determined individual refute the discouragement of the crowd. The executive must develop the ability to rationally and knowledgeably reach decisions and then go ahead—regardless of the "impossibility" of his goal.

Not long ago, I was forced to demand the resignation of a top-level executive in one of my companies. Although he was intelligent, hard-working and experienced, this man had a signal weakness that proved fatal to his career—and which, in time, might well have proved fatal to the company. He simply could not distinguish between the possible and the impossible—and his myopia extended to matters large and small.

Typical of his costly blunders was his tendency to undertake tasks which he should have realized were patently impossible to fulfill. Also typical were his ebulliently optimistic —and completely unrealistic—estimates of the time it would take to carry out an assignment or to complete a project.

"Yes, we can do it," he'd promise with bland assurance—even though "it" could not be done. "I'll have everything finished for you in three days," he'd say confidently—even though he must have known three *weeks* would be required to perform the work in question.

Perhaps he was driven by some compulsive desire to impress people with promises. Maybe he was afflicted with some rare form of sophomania or counted on fortuitous miracles to achieve the impossibilities he was in the habit of promising so rashly. Whatever the reasons, he gradually dragged himself—and his associates, subordinates and superiors—down into a morass of totally impractical projects, backlogged work, canceled orders and incomplete programs that had to be abandoned with consequent financial loss to the company.

This executive's inability to distinguish between the possible and the impossible created chaos within the company and alienated its customers. Brought to book for his shortcomings, he again demonstrated his fatal myopia by failing to realize that one cannot indefinitely hide one's mistakes behind glib excuses or displays of histrionics. He indulged freely in both in a futile effort to save the job he had already proved he could not possibly handle.

I believe it was La Rochefoucauld who first argued that "nothing is impossible." In my opinion, this is sheer nonsense and I flatly reject the theory, noting that even La Rochefoucauld felt it advisable to later amend his adage to read: "Few things are impossible in themselves."

I'm inclined to cock a skeptical eye at even this revised version. However, rather than further disparage the good Duc de La Rochefoucauld's philosophies, I'll assume that our definitions of the word "few" differ greatly and let it go at that. In any event, he was referring to matters on a more esoteric plane—while I am concerned with the hard-fact specifics of everyday living and particularly of business.

It is my opinion—and it has been my experience—that there are vast numbers of things which are impossible and that one is very likely to encounter them frequently in the business world. I firmly believe that one of the most valuable assets a businessman or executive can possess is the ability to study and weigh all the factors in a given situation and determine what is feasible and what is not—in short, to distinguish between the possible and the impossible. The ability is seldom innate; rather, it is acquired and developed. With it, an individual's chances of achieving success are greatly enhanced. Without it, he can go only so far—or fail altogether. Many an otherwise capable—or even great—man has failed because he lacked this capacity.

A comparison between Julius Caesar and Augustus Caesar indicates that Julius was basically the more able and gifted of the two. But Julius did not have the judgment and sense of proportion to separate the wheat of the possible from the chaff of the impossible—and this is what ultimately led to his downfall and assassination.

Augustus Caesar, on the other hand, recognized what were attainable goals, aimed for them and accomplished them. Consequently, he ruled much longer than Julius, and his overall accomplishments were much more constructive and lasting.

Napoleon Bonaparte was also an able and gifted individual—but he, too, was eventually destroyed by the malefic imp of the impossible. Napoleon—like Julius Caesar—was devoid of a sense of proportion, as evidenced by his disastrous invasion of Russia. The Compleat Megalomaniac, he blindly ignored the vast distances involved, the Russian climate and his own political weaknesses at home—all fairly obvious factors which doomed his campaign to failure long before his troops began their march to the east.

Now, a businessman who fails because he cannot distinguish between the possible and the impossible will not be stabbed to death in the boardroom by the company's directors—at least, not literally. Nor will he be exiled for the rest of his days to an island in the South Atlantic (unless, perhaps, the company happens to have a subsidiary plant or branch office there). Nonetheless, the practice of biting off more than he can properly chew will certainly prove calamitous to any executive's or businessman's career —and business.

But the converse is equally true, for the imp of the impossible is a perverse demon. The individual who is able to perceive the glint of the possible in a situation which outwardly appears to be fraught with insuperable obstacles is the most likely to reap the richest rewards. One does not have to look very far to find proof of this.

In the 1920s, self-taught engineer Robert G. LeTourneau's ideas for building huge earth-moving machines were widely considered to be impractical pipe dreams. LeTourneau, however, knew that he could actually produce the equipment his detractors predicted would be useless. He went on to build his giant machines and the nation's biggest earth-moving-machinery company—and to revolutionize the entire heavy-construction industry.

Reaching 65 in 1953, LeTourneau sold his business to Westinghouse Air Brake for a reported $31,000,000. He also agreed not to engage in manufacturing earth-moving machinery for the next five years. The consensus held that it would not be possible for him to get back into business again —not only because of his age, but also because he gave most of his money to a charitable foundation. LeTourneau confounded the consensus, however. By 1959—at the age of 71 —he was right back in business. He produced a revolutionary electrically powered, mobile offshore oil-drilling platform which, incidentally, the wiseacres had maintained "never could be built and wouldn't work even if it was." At last report, Robert LeTourneau's sales were said to be running in the neighborhood of $10,000,000 a year.

Few people, indeed, considered the Depression-era year of 1933 an auspicious one in which to start a new business. Among those who thought otherwise was young J. A. Ryder, who turned a deaf ear to the calamity howlers' warnings that any new business was bound to fail. Using $125 of his $155 "capital," Ryder bought a secondhand truck and went into business for himself. With an almost uncanny talent for perceiving the possible in the most unpromising times and situations, he went on to build his business. Within 25 years, he had created a trucking empire with an annual gross revenue that is said to exceed $85,000,000.

Shortly before V-E Day, First Lieutenant Melvin J. David was given a few days' leave from the front and sent to an Army rest center in Belgium. One afternoon, he noticed several Belgian villagers industriously twisting and welding scraps of heavy wire into various shapes. He saw that they were making lamp bases, stands and other utilitarian and decorative objects out of the wire they'd salvaged from nearby battlefields and the junk heaps of Allied supply dumps and depots.

The Belgians' activity gave David an idea. He saw the possibilities of using wire to mass-produce a wide range of industrial and consumer items. Discharged from the Army a year later, he went to Southern California and sought to translate his idea into commercially practical reality. Told that his ideas were unrealistic and impossible, he used his slender capital—$1500—to design and build his first machine and went into business. Today, Mel David's Melco

Wire Products Company is a thriving enterprise. The company produces everything from bosom-supporters for women's bathing suits to vital parts for jet aircraft—all made from wire.

The annals of American business have always been replete with such examples which prove that businessmen can achieve notable success by discerning the possibility of things which others consider impossible. The most significant inventions and advancements have been made—and the most successful businesses and largest fortunes have been created—in precisely this way.

I encountered—or perhaps I should say I stumbled into —a potentially possible "impossible" situation in 1940. My cousin, the late Hal Seymour, and I were vacationing in Mexico and stopped off in Acapulco. The climate, surroundings and sea being fine—and swimming being one of my favorite sports—we decided to stay awhile.

One day—and purely by accident—I met another tourist who exuberantly declared he'd discovered "the world's most beautiful beach" and asked me if I'd care to see it. I agreed that I would, almost backing out at the last minute when I learned we'd have to take a truck through some 15 miles of tropical forest to reach the spot. But I went anyway, clinging grimly to the side of an ancient truck that jounced and bumped along a crude dirt trail that looked as though it had been unused since the day it had been blazed by some wandering brontosaurus.

My first glimpse of Revolcadero Beach was ample compensation for the discomfort of the journey and balm for my bruises. My tourist friend hadn't exaggerated. It *was* the world's most beautiful beach. After a few more visits, I made up my mind to buy several hundred acres of the property and build a luxury resort hotel on the site.

Now, most people I know generally disagree about most things, but when I announced my intentions to buy and build at Revolcadero Beach, their reactions were uniquely unanimous.

"Impossible!"

The reasons they gave for considering my proposal impossible were legion—and, I must admit, ostensibly reasonable. The land I wanted to buy was completely undeveloped;

it would cost a fortune merely to clear it. There were no roads and no utilities; these would have to be built and provided at staggering cost. Revolcadero Beach was unknown and off the beaten path; people would not pay luxury-hotel rates in a resort that wasn't situated in a "fashionable" location. The type of resort I envisioned would need boat landings and a yacht basin; another fortune would be needed to build and dredge them. Europe was already at war—it was foolhardy to invest large sums in any foreign country . . .

So the objections ran—on and on. They varied in nature, but added up to a one-word total: "Impossible!"

I thought—I *knew*—the project was entirely possible. Development of the land alone would increase its value. The natural beauty of Revolcadero Beach and the construction of the type of hotel I envisioned there would be enough to make the resort "fashionable." Lower labor and material costs in Mexico would at least partially offset the added expense of building from scratch on virgin land. These and other considerations convinced me—and I bought the land. Pearl Harbor was attacked shortly afterward, and the United States entered World War Two. My plans for Revolcadero Beach were shelved for the duration.

It wasn't until 1956 that the Hotel Pierre Marques finally opened at Revolcadero Beach. When it did, the luxurious resort hotel proved to be all I'd anticipated and its instant success exceeded all hopes—another "impossible" project that was 100-percent possible from the beginning. There have been many others—large and small—before and after.

Back in the 1920s, a drilling bit that twisted off in a hole generally was a serious, expensive headache. Days, even weeks, were spent fruitlessly "fishing" for the bit. Meanwhile, the hole could not be drilled deeper, costs continued to mount up and frequently the oil for which one was drilling would be drained off by nearby wells.

"Fishing" was accepted as the only possible remedy for a twist-off; there seemed to be no feasible alternative. Then, in 1927, a company in which I held an interest had a twist-off on a Santa Fe Springs, California, drilling site. Several weeks were wasted while the crew "fished" for the bit. Thinking any possible new approach better than none, I went to a stoneyard hard by the nearest cemetery, where I bought a six-foot-long marble shaft and had one end cut to taper. Returning with it to the drilling site, I told the drillers to throw it down the hole—which they did.

The simple expedient worked. The heavy granite shaft slammed the bit out of the way. Granite whipstocks have been used successfully in similar situations on innumerable occasions since then. In the oil industry, they're called "Paul Getty Specials."

In the 1940s, it was considered impossible to drill horizontally in the oil fields. I was far from convinced that it couldn't be done by a newly developed technique utilizing flexible curved tubing and a mud pump. Shortly after World War Two ended, I had experiments carried out on one of my properties.

The techniques was improved and refined in the course of these experiments and soon proved entirely practical and efficient. As a result, horizontal drilling is now fairly commonplace. Many once-difficult and costly drilling problems now can be solved quickly and economically.

Even as recently as 1957 many experts and observers in the oil industry maintained it was impossible to build an automated oil refinery. Tidewater built one that same year in Delaware and it has astounded even its designers by its trouble-free efficiency ever since.

In very recent years, various "authorities" have held that the oil-tanker market is glutted, making it impossible to operate a tanker fleet profitably. Getty interests maintain a large tanker fleet, find it quite possible to operate it at a tidy profit—and have more super-tankers on order.

All top businessmen I know have made their biggest strides up the success ladder because they were able to see the possible in what others rejected or ignored as the impossible. And, I add hastily and emphatically, they managed to avoid taking large steps backward because they *generally* were able to recognize the impossible and give it a wide berth. I emphasize the word "generally" because everyone makes some mistakes. No one's record is perfect.

I've spent more than one large sum drilling thousands of feet into the ground in the belief it was possible I would strike oil—only to bring in a bone-dry hole.

I've sold more than one lease because I thought it *impossible* to find oil on the property—and then learned to my sorrow that the next leaseholder thought otherwise, drilled a well and brought in a producer.

I've made many other mistakes and miscalculations—more of them than I'd care to remember on days when I'm wearing a tight collar. There aren't any 1.000 batters. If there were, baseball wouldn't be much of a game—and if businessmen always made the right decisions, business wouldn't be business, would it?

The point I'm driving at is that the successful businessman is the one who makes the right choice between the possible and the impossible more often than not. The seasoned businessman does not arrive at such decisions by haphazard guesswork. Nor does he decide one way or another because he has a hunch or a clairvoyant premonition. A great deal of careful thought and consideration goes into resolving the problem of the possible versus the impossible.

No, there aren't any inflexible rules or money-back-guaranteed formulae for determining whether something is feasible or not. If there were, the question would never come up. However, there *is* an ordered, logical method by which any given business situation can be studied and weighed—and by the use of which the risk of error is greatly reduced.

Confronted by the perverse imp of the impossible, the veteran businessman organizes his thinking and examines all aspects of the situation with meticulous objectivity. He does this by asking himself a series of questions, the most important of which follow:

What—precisely and in detail—is the situation, proposition or issue under consideration?

What is at stake—what are the costs, what are the minimum and maximum the company stands to gain and lose?

Are there any precedents and, if so, can they be considered valid and applicable in this instance?

What do other parties—buyers or sellers, brokers, competitors, customers, etc.—stand to gain or lose either way?

What are the *known* obstacles and difficulties the company faces if it goes ahead—and precisely how can they be overcome?

What other difficulties are likely to arise—and if they do,

what resources are available and what steps may be taken to cope with them?

Are *all* the facts known—could there be any additional, hidden pitfalls?

How long will it take to accomplish the objectives or goals in question if it is decided to proceed?

Would the company stand to gain more by devoting equal time and effort to something else?

Are the personnel who would be responsible for handling the matter fully qualified and dependable?

Once he has the answers to these questions, the businessman weighs them in the balance to determine whether the undertaking is possible or impossible. If the scales tip heavily in one direction or another, his choice is not hard to make. If, on the other hand, the plus and minus factors tend to balance, then he must use his judgment, sense of proportion—and even his business intuition—to decide.

The veteran businessman mentally goes through this check list of questions automatically whenever there are any doubts about the practicality of a business situation. The young executive or beginner in business would do well under such circumstances to sit down with pencil and paper and actually list the questions and his debit-and-credit answers to them. The tyro is likely to obtain a clear—and sometimes entirely new and different—view of the problem confronting him if he sees the pro and con arguments and the various pertinent factors spelled out in black and white. He'll thus have before him a detailed inventory of the advantages and disadvantages, the potential rewards and potential dangers of all the elements forming the complete design.

Examining the over-all picture, the novice is very liable to see angles and aspects, flaws and strengths, expedients and alternatives, and potentials and pitfalls, which had previously eluded him or which he hadn't given much thought to before. Once it's all in front of him, he is like a chess player who studies his own pieces and those of his opponent on the board, then goes on to plan his tactics and strategy and anticipates the opponent's countermoves.

The chess analogy may well be carried further. Like the chess player, the executive or businessman can foresee which moves will "take pieces" from his opponent and which will cause him to "lose pieces" of his own. He'll be able to make a reasonable guess as to whether a certain gambit or attack will confer an advantage on him or his opponent. But, be this as it may, eventually he must make his decision. Is the situation possible—or impossible? Should he play, forfeit, or resign the game?

In business, as in chess, the final choice always and inevitably depends on the most important of all factors in any situation—the judgment of the individual concerned.

Possible—or impossible? When you are in business, it's up to *you* to decide.

PART THREE

The Value of Dissent, Culture
and Nonconformity

THE
VANISHING
AMERICANS

I recently had occasion to give a dinner party in London
for a rather widely assorted group of friends and acquaintances. Among the guests was an outspoken Socialist I've
known for many years. When the table conversation lagged,
he seized the opportunity to deliver a political monolog, expressing views which were more than slightly left of center.

To my amusement, one of my other guests, a vacationing
American businessman, later felt constrained to ask me how
I, a "leading Capitalist," could tolerate the presence of such
a wild radical at my dinner table.

"Aren't you afraid to have a man like that around you,
spouting all those dangerous theories?" he asked.

Keeping a straight face, I tried to explain that Socialism
is an entirely respectable political ideology in Great Britain,
adding, for what I hoped was proper snob-appealing emphasis,
that Socialists are even received at Buckingham Palace by
Her Majesty, the Queen.

I assured my worried fellow countryman I didn't really
consider the theories we'd heard expounded at all dangerous.
I said I hoped my own convictions weren't built on such
shifting foundations that a ten-minute tirade by a Socialist
zealot could undermine them or corrupt me.

My arguments did not appear to make very much of an impression. I strongly suspect the jittery businessman went away thinking that at best I had been contaminated by exposure to a subversive alien ideology and at worst had turned into one of those parlor pinks he'd heard so much about. Quite plainly, the man is one of the unfortunately far-too-numerous Americans who seem to have lost their perspective and sense of humor and fair play in recent years. They've developed a tendency to automatically equate dissension with disloyalty. They view any criticism of our existing social, economic and political forms as sedition and subversion.

Now, I am most certainly neither parlor nor any other shade of pink. It hardly seems necessary for me, of all people, to say that I'm vigorously opposed to government ownership of industry, that I'm an energetic exponent of the free-enterprise system. I can't imagine myself comfortable under a Socialist regime. Nor can I imagine such a regime looking upon me with much tolerance.

The political implications of the anecdote I've cited are purely incidental and coincidental. I used it solely to illustrate a manifestation of what I, for one, have observed to be a contemporary American phenomenon and which, to my mind, is disturbing, deplorable and truly dangerous. I'm referring to the growing reluctance of Americans to criticize, and their increasing tendency to condemn those who, in ever dwindling numbers, will still voice dissent, dissatisfaction and criticism.

Let me make it quite clear that I hold no special brief for any particular ideology, party, group or school of thought which might want or seek to bring about changes of any kind in our manners, mores or institutions. I am not a reformer, crusader, social philosopher, political or economic theorist. I do, however, consider myself enough of a realist to appreciate that this is not—and never has been and never will be—the best of all possible worlds. The concept that any *status quo* is perfect and permanent, that one must under no circumstances raise questions, voice doubts or seek improvements can only produce complacency, then stagnation and finally collapse. It does no good to pretend there is never anything wrong anywhere, for there is always something—be it big or little—wrong everywhere. Individuals and civilizations can only strive for perfection. It is highly unlikely that they will ever achieve it.

Very often it remains for the dissenter to point out that which is wrong. He is a skeptic who doubts, questions and probes—and hence is more likely to recognize lacks, weaknesses and abuses than are his complacent neighbors. The dissenter is also more alert and sensitive to the winds of impending change. He is thus frequently a prophet of the inevitable, who cries for action or change while there is yet time to take action and make changes voluntarily.

Such famed American dissenters of the past as Ida Tarbell, Lincoln Steffens, William Allen White and H. L. Mencken were labeled muckrakers and much worse by some of their contemporaries. Yet, they were given fair hearing. No one seriously suggested muzzling them. No one felt afraid of being exposed to their views. Their biting commentaries, hard-hitting denunciations and exposés helped bring about many needed changes and improvements which even the most antediluvian conservative of today will admit had to be made and, once made, were universally beneficial.

But even if the dissenter is a false prophet and cries of perils or problems which do not really exist, he still performs an important and valuable service to society. He adds spice, spirit and an invigorating quality to life. He may create naught but controversy, but if he is allowed to speak, is heard and answered, he has served to stir the imaginations of others.

Years ago, there were many ruggedly individualistic dissenters on the American scene. They were never hesitant to disagree with minorities or with the majority. They aimed their barbs at vital questions of the day. They expressed their opinions fearlessly, no matter how unpopular those opinions might have been. The voice of dissent has died away to a barely audible whisper. Present-day specimens of the vanishing breed are generally timorous and emasculated parodies akin to the medieval pedants who debated the question of how many angels could dance on the head of a pin.

Today's dissenters mainly focus their attention and expend their energies on the most inconsequential of trivia. Where the Ida Tarbells and H. L. Menckens made frontal assaults on fortresses, they snipe at houses of cards. Allegedly serious intellectuals quibble endlessly over such ridiculous trivialities as the artistic merit versus the political implications of a mural on the wall of a rural post office. In the meantime, the public is lulled into a perilous somnolence, spoon-fed pap and palpable untruths, many of which are turned out by special-interest and pressure groups and well-organized propaganda machines.

It is hardly surprising that the public mind is dulled and forced into a narrow mold which allows no room for consideration of the day's important issues. Let a semiliterate disc jockey's contract be terminated—for however valid the reason—and his former employers are promptly deluged by furious letters, telegrams and telephone calls expressing protest at the "injustice" and "persecution." On the other hand, if a pressure group of dubious motive forces the resignation of a distinguished public servant, there are very few protests from the citizenry.

If a motion-picture fan magazine casts aspersions on the dramatic talents of some glandular starlet, the result is instant, widespread reaction from a partisan public. But when a vital piece of legislation is pending before a state legislature or the United States Congress, the matter is usually ignored by the overwhelming majority of citizens. It remains for self-seeking pressure groups and professional lobbyists to inform the lawmakers of the public's attitudes and opinions on the bill in question. The stagnant waters of indifference and apathy are deep.

Some of our newspapers and magazines are more concerned with the welfare of their advertisers than they are with the dissemination of news and the discussion of matters of lasting importance. I recall a recent edition of one well-known newspaper that devoted two fully and lavishly illustrated pages to an article purporting to prove that *Happier Gelatin Molding Makes for a Happier Home Life*. The same issue gave a three-paragraph report on a government crisis in a Latin American Republic, dispensed with a far-reaching change in Civil Defense policy in 11 lines, and allotted a scant half column to a résumé of legislative action taken that week in the state capitol.

Editorial policies? "It's rapidly reaching the point where you're allowed to take a strong stand in favor of mothers, babies and stray dogs, and against crime and spitting in the streets—and that's about all," a veteran newspaper editor complained bitterly to me not long ago. This, of course, is obviously an angry man's extravagant overstatement. Nonetheless, it should be painfully apparent to any regular newspaper reader that there is at least some truth to what he says.

But newspapers and magazines are by no means the only —nor even the worst—offenders. Radio, television, motion pictures, popular books—all contribute their very considerable share to the conditioning process that leads to the stultification of thought and the stifling of dissent on all but the most banal levels. The extent to which some of these media will go to avoid controversy and to protect their own narrow interests is often incredible. It is graphically illustrated by a story I heard recently from a disgusted radio network executive. It appears that a large radio station killed a broadcast by a noted clergyman who was to have delivered a 15-minute talk on *The Sanctity of Marriage*.

Why was the cleric ruled off the air? The president of a firm which bought considerable advertising air time from the station was then involved in a noisy divorce scandal. The radio station's management was terrified lest this sponsor think the clergyman's remarks were directed at him!

It is, perhaps, significant that some of the most incisive and devastating commentaries on our contemporary manners, mores and institutions are being made today by nightclub comedians of the so-called sick school. This would seem to indicate that, to be heard, the present-day critic must sugarcoat his bitter pills, but that, even when he does, there is at least implied disapproval of his dissent. Otherwise, why would the public label his cutting, ironical commentaries as "sick"?

I contend there is nothing sick about dissent and criticism. There is a great need for both in our present-day society. I firmly believe that now, as never before in our history, it is essential that not only our intellectuals, but also our average citizens question, doubt, probe, criticize and object. The stifling of dissent is not only a negation of our constitutional guarantees of free speech, but also a renunciation of the most basic and precious of democratic principles. Only if there are open discussions and arguments based on uninhibited criticism

123

can there be an end to the growing trend toward complacency. And only when complacency disappears will it be possible for the United States to fully exert and exploit its vigorous, individualistic drive to achieve progress, betterment—and world leadership.

In a free society, nothing that in any way affects the lives or welfare of the public at large should ever be immune from examination and criticism. Be it our foreign policy, labor-management relations, educational system, or whatever, there is always justification and need for continuing, critical scrutiny.

As long as I've mentioned three specific areas of public interest, let's use them as examples and give each a quick glance. Let's begin by taking a single facet of our foreign policy to illustrate my point. Much time, money and energy are being expended in efforts to spread the American credo and to sell the American way of life abroad. Huge sums have been spent to build roads in countries that have few automobiles. Our Government has paid for the erection of giant office buildings in lands where the people live in mud huts. Costly exhibitions have been held in underdeveloped countries to show American refrigerators, television sets, electric ranges and wall-to-wall carpeting. We accept all these things as everyday commonplaces of our lives; but the average citizen of the countries in which we boast about our material wealth looks upon all such objects as unattainable—and often incomprehensible—luxuries.

This does not appear to be a very sensible mode of making friends of people who are underfed, poorly clothed and badly housed, unless we offer them definite, immediately workable programs whereby they can obtain these luxuries. It is almost inconceivable that some of our foreign-aid administrators have failed to see these self-evident truths. Nonetheless, there were many who failed to see them and, for all I know, there still are those who are constitutionally unable to view the problem in proper perspective.

This and other forms of blindness have handicapped America's ambitious and commendable programs for making friends and helping less fortunate people in foreign countries. Instead of giving those people hope and confidence, our representatives have frequently done nothing but emphasize the contrast between the host country's poverty and America's riches. Thus, the net result has been to increase resentment and to widen the gulf between backward nations and ourselves.

These situations and conditions have existed for quite a number of years. Yet, until very recently, it was considered at best very bad taste and at worst subversive to raise any questions about the omnipotence of those who directed our overseas aid programs.

As for American labor-management relations, some businessmen are still living figuratively in the long dead and unlamented days of public-be-damned laissez faire Capitalism. They resist any forward stride that may better the workingman's lot. In short, they consider labor as their natural enemy, rather than as their natural ally in a common effort. On the other hand, quite a number of labor leaders have ceased being labor leaders. Instead, they've become executives in a new and independent industry called labor. This form of labor has but one apparent aim: to compete with business and industry and to make things as difficult and unprofitable as possible for them.

Clearly, there are errors and abuses on both sides of the labor-management fence. Yet, anyone who criticizes management will quickly have the wrath of manufacturers' groups down on his head. He who criticizes labor or its leaders will have the full fury of labor groups and organizations to contend with. In the former case, he will be reviled as a radical. In the latter, he will be accused of being a reactionary. Consequently, there are few who are willing to criticize both sides freely and objectively. There remains only the highly prejudiced criticism of one side by the other.

Our educational system? A shocking percentage of our high school and college graduates are deficient in reading, writing and simple arithmetic. Their knowledge of geography is weak, of history, woolly and muddled. There is obviously something wrong with our educational system. It is not beyond the realm of possibility that there might even be something wrong with at least some of our schoolteachers. But heaven help anyone daring to express such heretical views.

Through some weird process of brainwashing, the public has come to believe that our schools are sacrosanct, beyond criticism or question. As for our teachers, they have been endowed with sublime qualities; they are pictured as long-suffering, overworked and underpaid martyrs sacrificing themselves on the altars of education. Any criticism of either schools or teachers brings a storm of abusive protest. Teachers' groups—and, egged on by them, parent-teacher associations—are quick to counterattack. The critic is characterized as an ogre who hates children and wishes to destroy civilization and bring about a return of the Dark Ages.

According to U.S. Office of Education figures, American schoolteachers' salaries have risen more than 1000 percent in the last 50 years or so. The average schoolteacher's salary today is over $4000 per year. Would anyone in his right mind say that the quality of our educational standards has risen comparably—or risen at all—in the last half century?

Now, I did not choose these three examples because I have any particular axes to grind. I do not say that our foreign policy is bad, nor even that it necessarily needs any major overhaul. I am not trying to blame either capital or labor for any economic ills. In no way do I wish to imply that I believe all our schoolteachers are incompetent or undeserving of high praise or pay. I chose the examples at random, merely to point out the fallacy of thinking that everything is always all right everywhere. There are always many things that require investigations, critical examination and evaluation—and then possibly change and improvement—in all areas of our society.

The public at large cannot allow itself to be swayed from seeking needed reforms by entrenched bureaucrats, selfish minority groups or organizations which have their own, and far from altruistic, reasons for wishing to preserve the *status quo*. In order that our society and its institutions may be strengthened there must be dissent. There must be dissenters who will seek out and point out the faults and abuses which exist or may develop.

"But most people today feel they can't afford to be dissenters," a moderately successful manufacturer declared to me recently. "They're afraid they'll lose their jobs, customers or profits if they try to buck powerful special-interest groups. You've got to be a multimillionaire to feel secure enough to speak out these days."

It so happens that I *am* a multimillionaire, but I'd hate to think it is for this reason alone that I can be a dissenter if I choose to be one. I don't believe it's true. I feel that the real reason there has been so little dissent of late is that Americans have been far too satisfied with their lot and with their achievements. We have all grown indifferent and complacent. Being too comfortable, we haven't wanted to see, say or hear anything which might disturb the bovine tranquillity of our rosy existence.

But I sense a strong wind of change in the offing. I'm of the opinion that America and its people are awakening to the realization that the lotus-eating binge is over. The hangover is already beginning to hurt—but it is having a highly beneficial effect. Through bleary eyes, we start to see the grave errors and deadly dangers in the "all is well and could not be better" thesis so long peddled by some of our leaders and the drumbeaters of Madison Avenue. I'm convinced the American people are ready to reclaim their minds and their nation, to take them back from the pressure groups, selfish minorities and hucksters to whom they lost them by default in recent years. I predict the vanishing American dissenters will soon reappear on the American scene and will once again make themselves heard—and will once again be given fair hearing. It will be a pleasure and a great relief to welcome them back. The nation's future will be brighter—and far more secure—for the return of the breed!

THE
EDUCATED
BARBARIANS

A big-circulation European magazine recently published a cartoon which depicted a camera-draped American tourist and a tourist-guide standing in front of some Greek temple ruins. "First World War or Second?" the caption had the American asking.

Although this may not sound very funny to you or me, the cartoon was widely reprinted all over the Continent. Countless Europeans laughed heartily at what they considered a telling lampoon of the typical American tourist. While foreigners have long acknowledged and acclaimed American leadership—and even supremacy—in science and technology, they have often been highly amused by the cultural illiteracy so often displayed by Americans and particularly by American men.

The curator of a famous French art museum tells me that he can instantly single out most American men in even the largest and most heterogeneous crowds that come to his galleries. "It's all in their walk," he claims. "The moment the average American male steps through the doors, he assumes a truculently self-conscious half-strut, half-shamble that tries to say: 'I don't really want to be here. I'd much rather be in a bar or watching a baseball game.'"

In my own opinion, the average American's cultural shortcomings can be likened to those of the educated barbarians of ancient Rome. These were barbarians who learned to speak —and often to read and write—Latin. They acquired Roman habits of dress and deportment. Many of them handily mastered Roman commercial, engineering and military techniques—but they remained barbarians nonetheless. They failed to develop any understanding, appreciation or love for the art and culture of the great civilization around them.

The culture-shunning American male has been a caricaturists' cliché for decades, at home as well as abroad—and with good reason. The traditional majority view in the United States has long seemed to be that culture is for women, longhairs and sissies—not for 100-percent, red-blooded men. Thus, it is hardly surprising that American women are generally far more advanced culturally than American males.

Because I spend much of my time abroad, I have many opportunities to observe my countrymen's reactions to the highly refined cultural climates of foreign countries. Frankly, I'm frequently shocked and discomfited by their bland lack of interest in anything that is even remotely cultural in nature. A graphic—and, I fear, all too representative—example of what I mean can be found in the story of a meeting I had with an old friend in London some time ago. My friend, a wealthy U.S. industrialist, stopped off in London en route to the Continent. He telephoned me from his hotel, and we arranged to have lunch together. After we'd eaten, I proposed that we spend a few hours visiting the Wallace Collection. I knew my companion had never seen this fabulous trove of antique furniture and art. As for myself, I was eager to revisit it and once again enjoy seeing the priceless treasures exhibited there. My friend, however, practically choked on the suggestion.

"Good Lord, Paul!" he spluttered indignantly. "I've only two days to spend in London—and I'm not going to waste an entire afternoon wandering around a musty art gallery. You can go look at antiques and oil paintings. *I'm* going to look at the girls at the Windmill!"

Then, I recall the dismal tableau enacted in my Paris hotel lobby not long ago when I played host to two American couples visiting Paris for the first time. I stood silently to one side while the husbands and wives argued about what they wanted to do that evening.

The ladies wanted to attend a special nighttime showing of a contemporary sculpture collection that had received high praise from all art critics. The husbands objected vehemently.

"Hell, I've already seen a statue!" one of the men snorted. "Let's go to a night club instead!"

The other man agreed enthusiastically. The wives capitulated, and I, being the host, submitted to the inevitable with as much grace as possible under the circumstances. As a consequence, we all spent the evening in an airless, smoke-filled cabaret exactly like every other airless, smoke-filled cabaret anywhere in the world, listening to a fourth-rate jazz band blare out background noise for a fifth-rate floorshow.

Now, I have nothing against cabarets, jazz bands or floorshows. I enjoy all three—provided they're good and provided I don't have to live on a steady diet of them. But I certainly can't understand why so many Americans will travel thousands of miles to a world cultural center such as Paris and then spend their time night clubbing.

Countless experiences similar to these I've related have led me to believe that a comparison between modern American men and the educated barbarians of ancient Rome is not so terribly far-fetched after all. I've found that the majority of American men really believe there is something effeminate— if not downright subversively un-American—about showing any interest in literature, drama, art, classical music, opera, ballet or any other type of cultural endeavor. It is virtually their *hubris* that they are too "manly" and "virile" for such effete things, that they prefer basketball to Bach or Brueghel and poker to Plato or Pirandello.

Unfortunately, this culture phobia is not an aberration peculiar to the uneducated clods in our society. It is to be found in virulent forms even among highly successful and otherwise intelligent and well-educated individuals. I've heard more than one man with a Phi Beta Kappa key glittering on his watchchain proclaim loudly that he "wouldn't be caught dead" inside an opera house, concert hall or art gallery. I'm acquainted with many top-level businessmen and executives with Ivy League backgrounds who don't know the difference between a Corot and a chromo—and couldn't care less.

The "anticulture" bias appears to thrive at most levels of American society. It is reflected in a thousand and one facets of American life. The nauseating, moronic fare dished out to radio, television and motion picture audiences—and presumably relished by them—is one random example. The comparatively sparse attendance at museums and permanent art exhibitions is another. Only a tiny percentage of the population reads great books or listens to great music. It's doubtful if one in ten Americans is able to differentiate between a Doric and an Ionic column. Save for amateur theatrical groups or touring road companies, the legitimate theater is rare outside New York City.

Americans like to boast that the United States is the richest nation on earth. They hardly seem to notice that in proportion to its material wealth and prosperity, the American people themselves are culturally poor, if not poverty-stricken.

The far-reaching and powerful influence of traditional American culture-shunning was, I think, illustrated quite clearly during the 1960 Presidential campaign. The music editor of the U.S. magazine *Saturday Review* queried both Presidential candidates for their answers to two questions:

1. Are you in favor of establishing a post of Secretary of Culture with Cabinet rank?

2. To what extent do you believe the Federal Government should assist in the support of museums, symphony orchestras, opera companies and so on?

According to published reports, both candidates rejected the idea of creating a Cabinet post for a Secretary of Culture. Neither seemed to think that Federal aid to domestic cultural activities, institutions and projects should be extended much beyond that which is already being given to the Library of Congress and the National Gallery.

Now, by no means do I intend this as a criticism of either our late President John F. Kennedy or of Mr. Richard M. Nixon. I rather imagine that their replies were made on the advice of their political counselors who doubtless warned them to tread carefully and avoid having any fatal "longhair" labels attached to their names.

As far as the first question is concerned, I hardly feel myself qualified to argue its pros and cons. It is not for me to judge whether a Secretary of Culture would be good or bad for the nation. I am, however, a taxpayer. As such, I cannot help but feel that a few Federal millions spent on cultural activities would be at least as well spent as the countless tens of millions lavished each year on bureaucratic paper-shuffling operations. Certainly all of our citizens would derive much greater benefits from such expenditures than they do from the costly pork-barrel projects to be found in almost every Federal budget.

The United States is the only major nation on earth that does not support its cultural institutions to some degree with public funds. True, the Federal Government has, in recent years, spent large sums to send artists, musicians, entire art exhibits, symphony orchestras and theatrical and dance troupes on globe-girdling junkets to spread American culture abroad for propaganda purposes. These are, of course, valuable projects which do much to raise American prestige in foreign lands. It is a grotesque paradox that the same Federal Government will not spend a penny to spread culture in America and thus raise the cultural level of our own people!

It strikes me that there is an Alice in Wonderland quality to whatever reasoning may lie behind all this. I am neither a politician nor a government economist. But it seems to me that if the Federal Government is legally obligated to see that the nation's citizens have pure foods, transcontinental highways and daily mail deliveries, then it has at least a moral obligation to see that they have the opportunities and facilities for cultural betterment.

Only one tenth of one percent—a one-thousandth fraction —of the annual Federal budget would be sufficient to finance a vast program of support for cultural institutions and activities throughout the country. It is hardly overpricing the value of our cultural present and future to say that they are well worth at least one thousandth of our Federal tax dollars!

History shows that civilizations live longest through their artistic and cultural achievements. We have forgotten the battles fought and the wars won by ancient civilizations, but we marvel at their architecture, art, painting, poetry and music. The greatness of nations and peoples is in their culture, not in their conquests. Themistocles is given only a line or two in most history books. Aristophanes, Aeschylus, Phidias, Socrates—all of whom lived in the same Century as Themistocles—are immortals. The edicts and decrees of the Caesars are largely forgotten. The poetry of Horace and Virgil lives on forever. The names of the Medicis, Sforzas and Viscontis gain their greatest luster from the patronage these noble families gave to Da Vinci, Michelangelo, Raphael and other unforgettable artists. What are Gneisenau and Scharnhorst in comparison to their countrymen and contemporaries: Beethoven, Schubert, Goethe and Heine? Surely, the moral should be obvious even to the most stubborn of culture shunners among today's Educated Barbarians.

Nonetheless, entirely too many American men insist that they can see no reason for developing any cultural interests or appreciation of the arts. Some say they "haven't time" for cultural pursuits. Yet, week after week, they will spend dozens of hours at country clubs, loafing here or there, slumped in easy chairs in their homes, staring blankly at the vulgar banalities that flash across the screens of their television sets.

I've found that a disheartening number of businessmen and executives—young and old—obstinately maintain that "business and culture don't mix." They cling to the notion that businessmen have neither the temperament nor the patience to understand and appreciate anything "artistic." They seem to fear that participation in cultural activities would somehow "soften" them and make them less able to cope with the harsh realities of the business world. Without doubt, these are the weakest and most fallacious of all arguments.

The world's most successful commercial and industrial leaders have always been noted as patrons of the arts and active supporters of all cultural activities. There are also innumerable proofs that commercial and industrial development, far from being incompatible with cultural progress, actually gives culture its strongest forward impetus. It can be shown that the arts have always flourished most vigorously in prosperous, highly commercialized and industrialized nations.

One excellent example of this is provided by the Republic of Venice, which dominated the commerce of Europe and Asia for nearly eight centuries. The Venetian traders were as shrewd and as materialistic as any the world has ever known.

The Venetians were also crack industrialists, mastering production-line techniques more than six hundred years before the first assembly line made its appearance in the United States. The gigantic arsenal at Venice was geared to turn out at least one fully equipped, seagoing ship a day on an assembly line that began with the laying of the vessel's keel and finished with the arming and provisioning of the ship.

The Venetians were hard-headed, profit-conscious merchants and manufacturers. All things considered, they faced far more risks and problems in their day-to-day operations than any modern businessman. Nevertheless, these were the men who were responsible for the building of the Doges' Palace, the Golden Basilica of St. Mark, the great *palazzi* along the Grand Canal and uncounted other magnificent structures which they filled with works of incomparable beauty.

It was in and for "commercial" Venice that Tintoretto, Titian, Veronese and many other masters produced their greatest works. The canal-laced city of tough-skinned merchants and manufacturers became an artistic wonder of the world—and so it remains even to this day. The beauty and esthetic grandeur of Venice have endured—monuments not only to the artists who created the beauty, but also to the businessmen at whose behest it was created.

In modern times, cultural progress has certainly kept pace with industrial and commercial expansion in such nations as England, France, Italy and Sweden—to name only a few. Neither businessmen nor the populace as a whole in any of these countries is taking any less interest in cultural activities today than they did years, decades or generations ago. Quite to the contrary. It is evident that, although their lives have grown more complex and their pace of living has been greatly accelerated, they are still packing the art galleries, museums, concert halls, theaters and opera houses.

These people have learned a lesson it would be well for many Americans to study. They have learned that culture bestows many rewards and benefits—among them a better, more satisfactory life, great inner satisfaction and mental and emotional refreshment and inspiration.

Americans traveling abroad are often startled to hear rubbish collectors or street sweepers singing operatic arias or humming the themes of symphonies or concertos as they go about their work. If they happen to know the language of the country they are visiting, American tourists are even more surprised when—as frequently happens—they hear restaurant waiters or hotel employees arguing heatedly among themselves over the relative merits of various Impressionist painters or classical dramatists.

Many Americans who go overseas on business are nonplused to find their foreign counterparts interspersing their business conversations with references—and quotations—from great authors, poets, playwrights and philosophers about whom the Americans have only the haziest knowledge.

Saddest of all are some American businessmen I've encountered in Europe who went abroad to buy or invest and expected European manufacturers to entertain them in the best accepted Madison Avenue tradition—with wild nights on the town. I've listened with a straight face and, I hope, with an adequately sympathetic expression to the woeful recitals of several of these men who wailed that instead of the anticipated champagne-soaked orgies, they found themselves being taken to the opera or the ballet.

What I'm driving at is that the average man in most civilized foreign countries—be he laborer or industrial magnate—takes a keen interest in and has a deep appreciation of all forms of cultural and artistic expression.

There are, I suppose, several principal reasons for the indifference—if not open hostility—of the majority of American men toward all things that come under artistic or cultural headings. Some of the roots can be found in our Puritan heritage. Early American Puritans, hewing to their stern, super-Calvinist doctrines, equated art with depravity, branded most music as carnal and licentious, shunned literature other than religious tracts or theological discourses and condemned virtually all cultural pursuits as being frivolous and sinful. In the Puritan view, that which was not starkly simple and coldly functional was, *propter hoc*, debauched and degenerate.

Despite the fact that the Puritans were only a minority to begin with and were entirely engulfed by later infusions of non-Puritan stock into the American melting pot, the influence of the Puritan heritage on American thought and behavior can be noted even to this day.

Then, there is the Colonial and Revolutionary tradition which so many alleged authorities have quite incorrectly defined as having demanded a complete break with all that was European, including the "decadent" cultures of England and the Continent.

The founding fathers desired no such thing. They sought political independence from England and wished to eliminate monarchy and titled aristocracy from the American scheme. But most leading figures of the American Revolution hoped to preserve the cultural traditions of the Old World and to transplant the highly developed art and culture of England and Europe to the New World.

Benjamin Franklin, George Washington, John Adams—to mention only three—were all men of culture. Anyone who has ever visited Thomas Jefferson's home in Monticello must have been impressed by the flawless taste reflected in the architecture and furnishings of the house built by this man who read the classics in Greek and Latin.

But then, one need look no further than the architecture of the nation's capital to find refutation of the theory that the founders of the United States desired to discard foreign artistic and cultural influences. The Capitol Building and the White House, both designed soon after the Revolutionary War ended, are excellent examples. The Capitol Building is strongly reminiscent of St. Peter's Basilica in Rome. There is a startling resemblance between the main façade of the White House and that of the Duke of Leinster's home in Dublin, on which architect James Hoban based his designs for the Executive Mansion.

Despite the mass of incontrovertible proof to the contrary, there are still ultrapatriots and professional chauvinists who believe that the Colonial tradition entailed a repudiation of classical—and particularly European or foreign—art and culture. From this fallacious concept it is only a short step to the theory that *all* cultural activities are un-American and unsuited for red-blooded Americans.

As if these influences—the Puritan and what might be termed the pseudo-Colonial traditions—were not enough, the average American man's attitude toward culture has been further warped by the mythical mystique of the American frontier heritage. The rough-and-ready, generally unlettered and often uncouth, frontiersman long ago became the figure after which generations of American men would subconsciously pattern themselves. Believing that they are emulating praiseworthy qualities of their pioneer forebears, many U.S. males sneer at any art above the *September Morn* level and jeer at any music that cannot be played on a honky-tonk piano or twanged and scraped out by a self-taught banjo player and an amateur fiddler.

The figure of the two-fisted, fast-drawing and culture-hating frontiersman may be picturesque, but it is a misleading one.

There were many cultured men—and men who thirsted for culture—as well as barroom brawlers and gunslingers on the American frontier.

It is, perhaps, significant to note the examples provided by two rough, tough cities that played important roles in America's Westward expansion—San Francisco and Denver.

San Francisco's Barbary Coast and Denver's Holladay Street were probably the wickedest and wildest enclaves in all the wild, wild West. Even so, there were few Eastern metropolises that gave such quick and unstinting support to cultural projects as did San Francisco and Denver, even in their raucous infancy.

San Franciscans always showed an appreciation for music and art—even in the days when the city was a gold-rush-era Helldorado. There are very few metropolises in the United States today with higher general levels of taste and culture than San Francisco—and the city's cultural traditions go back well over a century.

Denver had its Occidental Hall and the Tabor Grand Opera House—the latter built by H. A. W. Tabor, as crude a character as can be found in American history. The Tabor Grand Opera House was a showplace of the West. Operas, concerts and lectures were given there—and Denverites packed the auditorium, listened attentively and, if contemporary accounts are to be believed, appreciatively.

I believe I am qualified to comment personally on the culture-shunning myth of the American frontier. My own forebears came to the United States in the Eighteenth Century. They were pioneers, mainly farmers, who came to America to build their futures in the wilderness. It was for one of them, James Getty, that Gettysburg, Pennsylvania, was named. Judging by the memorabilia these people left behind, they and large numbers of their contemporaries hungered for culture and knowledge in all forms. They read avidly, passing books—particularly the classics—from hand to hand. They dreamed of the day when they could have good oil paintings on the walls of the good homes they hoped to build. They tried to teach their children to appreciate and love fine literature, art and music.

My own father was born in 1855 on an Ohio farm—and a very poor and unproductive farm at that. His widowed mother was impoverished and life was anything but simple and easy. Yet, the thirst for intellectual and cultural betterment was great. My father worked his way through school and college, and one of his greatest sources of pride was his membership in the university's literary society.

I, myself, had a heaping helping of life on America's last frontier when, in 1904, my father, mother and I went to the Oklahoma Territory. Clapboard and raw-pine settlements had mushroomed overnight around newly discovered oil fields and newly established drilling sites. Most grown men habitually carried six-guns strapped to their waists; shooting affrays were everyday commonplaces.

The oil-field workers and wildcatters were certainly hard, tough and virile, but I can remember many of the toughest among them dressing up in their Sunday best and going to Oklahoma City or Tulsa to hear a touring opera company or a concert artist perform.

When they struck it rich, a great many oil men—I might even say most—bought or built homes and purchased paintings, sculpture and antique furniture and rugs for them. They also went East, to New York, to see the plays and hear the operas and concerts.

True, their tastes were seldom refined or matured—at least not at first. But the fact remains that these rugged, hardbitten men *did* thirst for artistic beauty, and they *did* take an active interest in and show appreciation for things cultural. By no means were they the culture-phobes that so many modern Americans think all frontiersmen and oldtimers were and whose imagined example they seek to emulate in order to prove themselves rugged, two-fisted all-male men.

There are other factors that help produce such a high proportion of educated barbarians among American men—but, regardless of the causes, the results are deplorable.

The saddest part of the whole situation is that the United States *does* possess outstanding cultural institutions and facilities. American symphony orchestras and opera companies are among the finest in the world. American museums and art galleries—public and private—have amassed some of the world's greatest collections of paintings, sculpture, tapestries, antique furniture—of art in all its forms from all historical periods.

The Educated Barbarians

Great music is available on phonograph records and recording tapes. Fine works by contemporary painters and sculptors and fine reproductions of the works of the masters are well within the reach of most Americans' pocketbooks. The great classics of literature are available in editions costing only a few cents per volume. Courses in art and music appreciation, literature, poetry and drama are offered, not only in the public schools and colleges, but also in adult education programs.

Tragically, only a comparatively tiny fraction of the population—and particularly of the male population—takes advantage of the myriad facilities and opportunities that are offered throughout the country.

Symphony orchestras and opera companies often end their seasons with staggering deficits. Few, indeed, are the art museums and galleries that can report regular heavy attendance. Countless record albums featuring the caterwaulings of some bosomy *chanteuse* or tone-deaf crooner are sold for every album of serious music that is purchased. Even greater numbers of lurid, ill-written novels are snapped up for every volume of serious literature that is bought. Save for a few sections of the country, cultural classes and courses seldom if ever have capacity enrollments. Teachers and professors who conduct such classes have told me that a course that should have 30 or 40 students enrolled in it will have only six or eight.

Americans, and especially American men, must realize that an understanding and appreciation of literature, drama, art, music—in short, of culture—will give them a broader, better foundation in life, and will enable them to enjoy life more, and more fully. It will provide them with better balance and perspective, with interests that are pleasing to the senses and inwardly satisfying and gratifying.

Far from emasculating or effeminizing a man, a cultural interest serves to make him more completely male as well as a more complete human being. It stimulates and vitalizes him as an individual—and sharpens his tastes, sensibilities and sensitivity for and to all things in life.

The cultured man is almost invariably a self-assured, urbane and completely confident male. He recognizes, appreciates and enjoys the subtler shadings and nuances to be found in the intellectual, emotional and even physical spheres of human existence—and in the relationships between human beings. Be it in a board room or a bedroom, he is much better equipped to play his masculine role than is the heavy-handed and maladroit educated barbarian.

It isn't necessary to force-feed oneself with culture nor to forsake other interests in order to experience the benefits and pleasures offered by cultural pursuits. One's preferences, tastes and knowledge should be developed slowly, gradually—and enjoyably. Culture is like a fine wine that one drinks in the company of a beautiful woman. It should be sipped and savored—never gulped.

THE
HOMOGENIZED
MAN

At odd moments, when sunk in contemplation of some cosmic navel, the vague suspicion that I am, at heart, an anarchist flashes through my mind. Not that any impulse to strew high explosives in palace gardens or parliamentary antechambers stirs within me; I certainly bear no malice whatsoever toward aged archdukes or young czarevitches.

My evanescent anarchistic tendencies are purely classical. I use the word anarchist in the sense in which it was understood by the ancient Greeks. They, of course, accepted the anarchist as a fairly respectable—if somewhat vehement—opponent of government encroachment on the individual's rights to think and act freely. It is in this sense that I glimpse myself as an anarchist—regretting the growth of government and the ever-increasing trend toward regulation and, worst of all, standardization of human activity.

I never dwell long on such thoughts, however, for no man relishes seeing himself as an anachronism clinging hopelessly to obsolete concepts. Being a realist, I am forced to concede that in the *guerre à outrance* between individual rights and government prerogatives, the latter have clearly emerged the victors.

Big government has been with us for quite some time—and it continues to grow bigger. The government administrator and "planner" and the electronic brain are inheriting what daily becomes more and more of a punch-card world. Led by big government—which, after all, sets the style—we are moving rapidly and inexorably into the era of the completely structured society, the bureaucrat's beehive utopia in which there will be just one great assonant buzz.

I, personally, find the prospect dismal, but I appreciate that what is a strait jacket for one man may well seem a loose-flowing toga to the next. Even such words as forward and backward are relative terms; their meanings depend on where one is standing before he starts to move. There are unquestionably many to whom the planned and ordered—if not very brave—new world of the future will appear as the safest of all possible havens.

Nonetheless, it should be plain to all that the completely structured society will impose increasingly severe restrictions on its members and will drastically change most—and quite possibly all—of our existing social and economic patterns. But then, these changes will not really be new—only final and complete. They have been taking place more or less gradually for a long time; the trend toward the structuring of society has been evident for centuries.

In the ancient Greek city-states, premiums were set on individuality in almost all things. But, with the emergence of the concept of empire, the movement toward uniformity was firmly established.

Within the Roman Empire, for example, such diverse things as laws, the administration of justice, fashions in wearing apparel and business practices became highly standardized. The civilization, customs, manners and mores exported by Rome impressed themselves—and were impressed upon—subjected and allied peoples, many classes among whom eagerly accepted and aped them. Temples, amphitheaters, dwelling places and other structures built by the Roman legions in the Empire's far-flung reaches were, save perhaps for size, virtually identical to like structures built in Rome. The artistic style and techniques apparent in a Second Century portrait bust found in a Roman ruin in Syria are practically indistinguishable from those to be seen in a Second Century bust dug from the banks of the Tiber.

It is not unreasonable to assume that if the Roman Empire had survived, the civilizations of Europe, the Middle East and North Africa might well have developed according to the prototypal patterns established by Rome. The Empire, however, collapsed. The ordered whole was shattered into myriad splintered fragments. Even Latin, long the language of Western civilization, was split into innumerable languages and dialects. With that, the trend toward standardization was temporarily halted. Countless highly individualistic tribal societies and minor principalities replaced strongly organized imperial government. The chaotic patchwork remained until, at last, the feudal system that had evolved during the Dark Ages finally withered and died. Then, with the re-emergence of strong central governments, a marked trend toward unification and standardization began again.

The movement has continued steadily throughout the last four or five hundred years. In more recent generations, burgeoning populations, multiplying social and economic problems and such other factors as vastly improved communications have strengthened the trend and caused it to move at a progressively faster pace. Today, the tendency toward standardization is evident almost everywhere on the globe. Native costumes have been largely discarded in many countries; the custom is to dress in Western-style clothing. A woman's dress fashion set in Paris one day is reported by press, radio and television on every continent within hours; within a week it has become the vogue throughout much of the world. There isn't much difference between the appearance of, say, refrigerators built in England and those manufactured in the United States, France, Italy or Germany. Let an architectural style catch on in one country, and you can be sure that it will become the rage in a dozen other countries in short order.

Today, the inherent nature of government in an increasingly complex civilization creates strong pressures toward systemization and standardization, which, in turn, serves to create vast bureaucratic complexes. In government (as in overgrown big-business corporations that have assumed government-style managerial practices) the attempt to establish rigid procedures for the most minute activities tends to guarantee imposition of a structured conformity. Needless to say, all this proves especially appealing to the type of job seeker and job holder who is bereft of courage and imagination and basks like some somnolent embryo in the amniotic comfort of a completely regulated life.

The bureaucratic mazes of government are self-perpetuating, self-propagating and given to mitosis—and they grow ever more intricate, unwieldy and ubiquitous. I do not suggest that there is a malevolent force behind any of this. It is simply the way things are, simply the way they have developed and continue to develop.

Our own country's history provides an illuminating example of how nations move toward the creation of a structured society. Originally 13 rather loosely federated states dedicated to the proposition that all government should be held to a minimum and individual liberty kept at a maximum, the United States has changed greatly since the Declaration of Independence was signed. Modern America is a country with national, state and local governments that are infinitely more powerful than was ever envisioned by our founding fathers. Today, the hand of government can be felt—regulating, prescribing, proscribing and standardizing—in almost every area of human activity.

True, our nation's citizens are as free as any people on the face of the earth, far more than most. But just *how* free are they? To what extent has government already encroached on their freedoms and their rights to life, liberty and the pursuit of happiness?

I think the average American would be astounded to realize how many commonplace things he may *not* do unless he maintains standards set by government and obtains permission from government to do them in the first place. I rather doubt that most people have ever stopped to think about it.

For example, the average American citizen cannot sell a bottle of beer, get married, go hunting or fishing, drive an automobile or even keep a dog for a pet without appropriate licenses from government. In most places throughout the United States, he cannot hold a parade, build a house or even add a bathroom to his home unless he first obtains permits to do these things from government. He must not operate so much as a pet shop, a boardinghouse or a soda fountain without licenses or permits from such government departments as police, health, fire and so on, ad bureaucratic infinitum.

From the moment he is born and his birth certificate is filled out and recorded, the average American is a marked human being. His life, habits and activities become the concern of numberless bureaucratic offices and agencies which register, enroll, scrutinize, supervise and regulate him and whatever he may do until the day he dies, and even after.

Our free American *must* be enrolled in school at a certain

age and must remain there for a prescribed period studying at least some prescribed subjects. Male members of the population must register with Selective Service boards. They remain eligible for military service for many years; if called, they must serve in the Armed Forces for a specified time. Most Americans—regardless of sex—must register with the agencies handling Social Security, workmen's compensation, income tax, census and other Federal, state, county, or city government bureaus.

Now, I hasten to make clear that I consider these requirements necessary and beneficial. Obviously there must be laws and standards in our complex civilization. Unrestricted hunting would quickly wipe out all game animals; unlicensed drivers would greatly increase the already appalling slaughter on our jammed streets and highways. An individual cannot be allowed to erect a slovenly shack where others have built fine homes; nor should he be allowed to operate a boardinghouse that is a firetrap or a menace to the health of its tenants. The nation's security in a troubled world depends on its armed forces, hence the need for Selective Service. Certainly no sane person would want to abolish the census. Government, law, control and regulation—and even concomitant bureaucracy—are essential if a nation of 190,000,000 people is to exist and function, if there is not to be utter chaos and eventual destruction.

I would like to repeat and make it very clear that I am no antigovernment reactionary. I do not maintain that the restrictions I have cited are undesirable. They are, in my opinion, entirely necessary, in that their purpose is to make life safer and more pleasant for all.

The issue is not that any of these manifestations are good or bad. The point is simply that they *are*, that they exist, are implemented and enforced, affecting all citizens. They are mentioned only as demonstrations of the extent to which we are already living in a regulated society.

Further proof may be found in the manifold ways in which government at all levels controls the nation's business and economy. Like it or not, the so-called free-enterprise system is not nearly as free as some might imagine. The Federal Government alone has some 30 *independent* regulatory agencies which wield great power and influence over practically every aspect of U. S. business.

Take, for example, the duties and responsibilities of just three of these agencies. The Interstate Commerce Commission fixes rates and grants franchises for railroads, barge lines, trucking and pipeline firms. The Civil Aeronautics Board sets airline routes, rates and safety standards. The Federal Communications Commission determines who may (or may not) operate radio or television broadcasting stations. In addition to such independent regulatory agencies, there are scores of other Federal bureaus and offices that exert influence and exercise varying degrees of direct and indirect control over the country's economy and business. Farm production is regulated through price supports, acreage controls and other methods—and the effects are felt not only by the farmer but by the produce trucker, food wholesaler, corner grocer and consumer as well. Government affects business activity and expansion by raising or lowering Federal Reserve discount rates, tariffs, taxes and by innumerable other means. Whatever it does in these directions is soon reflected in production and sales figures, employment statistics and price indexes.

In short, big government wields numberless big sticks over American business and the American economy. And, when I speak of big government, I do not mean the Federal Government alone. The various states—and even counties and cities —license, tax, inspect and regulate businesses within their jurisdictions. It should hardly be necessary to mention that it is but a short step from such economic regulation as exists at the present time to the establishment of a completely regulated economy. And—be it for better or for worse—all recognizable signs augur more, rather than less, economic regulation for the future.

With government setting the example, it is little wonder that many of the nation's citizens anticipate the seemingly inevitable and hasten to conform to standardized patterns. Business firms that establish their own bureaucracies and individuals who strive to be conformists are merely floating with the tide that is carrying our society toward final, top-to-bottom "structurization." There are abundant indications that this is in the offing, that the civilization that produced homogenized milk will soon produce the homogenized man.

The Homogenized Man

Not long ago, the Federal Government, acutely concerned over the shortage of scientific and engineering personnel in the United States, launched a program designed to encourage young people to become scientists and engineers. To date, the technique employed has been one that seeks to *impel* young people to choose these careers. Public statements by national leaders and other prominent persons and widespread publicity campaigns aim to make science and engineering attractive, to excite the imaginations of the young and to sell the idea of following such careers to students in high schools and colleges. Huge money grants are financing the expansion of training facilities at universities and colleges and are making it possible for these institutions to offer scholarships and fellowships on an unprecedented scale.

Now, all this is very necessary—and very much to the good. But, considering the trend, it should not be too difficult for any moderately imaginative person to visualize a day when government will no longer *impel*, but will *compel* individuals to enter certain professions or career fields.

One does not have to be a science-fiction addict to imagine how this might be accomplished in a fully programed society. Somewhere in a government building, an electronic computer whirs, calculating how many new physicians the country will require six years hence. The data obtained is fed into another machine which promptly spews out punch cards on which are recorded the names of the nation's high school seniors who made the highest scores on the medical section of the Standard Career Aptitude Test. Within a few days, the students receive their career-assignment notices through the zip-coded mails.

That such a system might prevail at some time in the future is no longer a fantasy. It is a distinct possibility. We have already passed the point of no return in our race to establish the structured society.

"But then, we are headed for regimentation!" the reader is quite likely to protest. Well, we are—and we aren't. I'll admit that at first glance, the difference between a structured society and a regimented one may not be too apparent. But there are differences—and very big differences, at that. Although I can hardly say that I would be overjoyed by the prospect of living in either, if forced to make a choice, I would most certainly take the former.

As defined by common usage, the regimented society is one produced by totalitarianism and dictatorship. It is created, operated and controlled by a selfish and cynical minority using ruthless methods and totally disregarding the rights, welfare and human dignity of the majority. In it, the majority exists solely to serve the ruling minority's ends and purposes. To me, at least, the regimented society implies all the classic appurtenances of dictatorship—terror, concentration camps—and the end to all human dignity.

On the other hand, the structured society, as I choose to understand it, is one that evolves with the consent—be it active or tacit—of the majority of its members. Although it is organized, regulated, standardized and programed, its goals are still to provide the greatest good for the greatest number without using oppressive measures against any. And, at least to these extents, the governing elements in such a society are benevolent and altruistic in their intents. They do not rely on rigged show trials or *Nacht und Nebel* decrees to govern.

Stated simply, the regimented society is the Orwellian nightmare, while the structured society is the do-good social theoretician's dull, monochromatic dream of utopia. The completely structured civilization will provide complete security for its members, quite literally from womb to tomb. The individual's needs will be defined, anticipated and met—not through his own foresight and abilities but by government experts and administrators. They will watch him—and watch over him. They will classify him, evaluate his potentials, assign him to his tasks, supervise his life, and press him into the mold they determine to be the one he fits or should fit. They will, of course, do these things for his "own good" and for the "good of society as a whole."

Theoretically, at any rate, there will be very little insecurity or want in this Erewhonian ants' nest. The individual will face few of the anxieties he is liable to encounter in a freely competitive society. His progress through life will be a measured journey up a neatly structured ladder. He will go from one faceless level to another, under constant surveillance by those appointed to guard the rungs. "A slot for everyone—and everyone in his slot," will be the guiding principle.

It all promises to be rather boring. Whatever else the structured society may or may not offer, it definitely will *not* offer the individual adventure or inspiration—and precious little challenge. He will plod slowly along in the groove provided him, knowing full well exactly what to expect at every step.

Many forces are at work to bring this era of the homogenized man ever closer. Each contributes its part in preparing the ground and the conditioning process which will make the majority accept its advent without a protesting murmur.

I've already dwelt at some length on the role played by government, which tends to impress the patterns it has adopted for its bureaucratic microcosms on the social macrocosm. Business, too, hastens the coming of the structured society—and, as a conceivable consequence, its own doom—by its ever-increasing tendency to overorganize, to place more emphasis on procedural rules than on production and to show more concern over committee meetings than customers.

Many businessmen who complain most about government's bureaucratic meddling are lost in bureaucratic labyrinths of their own making. Far too many wallow in organizational charts, administrative directives and quintuplicated memoranda, worrying more about doing their paperwork than about doing business.

Labor unions contribute their share by such attitudes as inflexible insistence that seniority rather than merit and efficiency be the yardstick by which eligibility for promotion is measured. Thus, the time server takes precedence and receives preference over the toiler.

Schools and colleges do their not-inconsiderable bit by producing overspecialized graduates whose knowledge and horizons are severely limited. An unfortunately large percentage of students leave their schools ready tailored to fit only the narrowest of grooves.

Individuals help accelerate the trend toward a programed social and economic system by their complacent, almost bovine, acceptance of it all. In many instances, they rush pell-mell to conform, to be the first to enjoy the dubious fruits they hope to find in the safely structured nirvana. Vast numbers have already anticipated the dawn of homogenized civilization, but there are still those who refuse to join the cults of the conformists, status seekers and organization men which form the super mystique of security at all costs.

One might well ask what, in an increasingly standardized society, dominated by standardizing and stultifying government, the individual can do to protect himself from becoming a homogenized man. In my opinion, there is much he can do.

In the first place, to be forewarned is to be forearmed. The man who wants to be an individualist, call his life his own and retain considerable freedom of will and action should be alert to those activities and courses of action which might lead him unwittingly into the trap of standardization. For instance, such comparatively simple things as the reading of newspapers and listening to the opinions of others—all with an open mind tempered with a bit of healthy skepticism—are a great help. Then, whenever the individual is confronted with the necessity of making a choice—be it in voting, choosing a career or a job, buying something, or whatever—the question of whether he wants (or thinks he wants) to do this or that should not be the only consideration governing the choice. The individual must also ask himself whether the choice will circumscribe his life or make him more susceptible to the forces in our society that tend to standardize people.

The would-be individualist will carefully examine his motives for wanting something and ask himself whether he is making his choice because it is safe, secure, easy. He will strive to accept or reject so that he will maintain as much mobility and personal freedom as possible. He will understand that however high the price of courage and self-determination, the rewards are ultimately far greater in terms of personal satisfaction than can be obtained by passively permitting himself to be trundled from infancy to decrepitude by governments and institutions which may indeed wish him well, but which throttle his individualism.

I am convinced there will always be those who reject any system that considers them as numbers, as code holes in a punch card. Admittedly, the completely structured society will be heaven on earth for the meek conformists and for those who lack imagination, initiative, self-confidence and self-respect. But there will always be individualists and they will always make their presence known as they assert their individuality. Such persons have always existed and will always exist, never content to have their lives systematized. Whatever the forces against them, they live their own lives and achieve their aims on their own.

I can't honestly say that I think the over-all outlook is very bright. I believe that more and more regulation, standardization and uniformity are virtually inevitable—if for no other reason than that populations and social and economic problems have become too complex to be coped with in any other manner.

There is, however, hope for any person who wants to remain an individual. He can assert himself and refuse to conform. He'll be on his own, that's true, but while he will not have the security enjoyed by those who do conform, there will be no limits to what he may achieve.

It shouldn't be very difficult for anyone to resist the temptation to force himself into the pattern of the structured man. One needs only to remember that a groove may be safe—but that, as one wears away at it, the groove becomes first a rut and finally a grave.

PART FOUR

The Art of Investment

THE
WALL STREET
INVESTOR

On Monday, May 28, 1962, prices of the New York Stock Exchange crumbled rapidly before an avalanche of sell orders. The Dow-Jones industrial average plunged nearly 35 points to register its biggest one-day drop in over 32 years. Crashing through the 600 level for the first time since 1960, it hit a day's low of 576.93.

By the end of the day, many big-board stocks were selling at prices from 30 to 80 percent below their 1962 highs. Shares traded on the American Exchange and over-the-counter markets followed suit and also went into nosedives. Headline writers were quick to respond to the developments being reported by the lagging ticker:

BLACK MONDAY PANIC ON WALL STREET
INVESTORS LOSE BILLIONS AS MARKET BREAKS
NATION FEARS NEW 1929 DEBACLE

Such were the scare heads that appeared on the front pages of the nation's newspapers after the New York Stock Exchange closed for the day. By the time later editions came off the press, experts and analysts, economists and pundits were offering their explanations, hindsight diagnoses and spur-of-the-moment prognostications. As is often the case in such situations, some of the second-guessers and crystal-ball gazers tried to gloss over the implications of the collapse, while others appeared to take an almost sadistic delight in prophesying even worse things to come.

Two days later, several newspapers and wire-service correspondents descended on me. They wanted to know my opinions and reactions and asked what I was doing because of the break in stock prices. I told them quite frankly that, while I sympathized wholeheartedly with anyone who had lost money because of market developments, I saw little if any reason for alarm and absolutely none for panic.

The over-all current business picture was favorable and, what was even more important, gave promise of getting better in the future. There was nothing basically wrong with the American economy nor the vast majority of companies whose stocks were listed on the New York Stock Exchange. In my view, some stocks had been grossly over-priced. Irrational buying had driven their prices to totally unrealistic levels. The May 28 break was an inevitable consequence.

I said that I felt the stock market was in a much healthier and certainly in a much more realistic position because of the long-needed adjustment of prices. As for what I was doing, the answer was simple. I was buying stocks.

"I'd be foolish *not* to buy," I explained to a young correspondent who looked as though he thought I'd taken leave of my senses by buying when everyone else seemed to be selling. "Most seasoned investors are doubtless doing much the same thing," I went on, feeling somewhat like a schoolmaster conducting a short course in the First Principles of Investment. "They're snapping up the fine stock bargains available as a result of the emotionally inspired selling wave."

Since the petroleum industry is the one I know best, I bought oil stocks. By the end of the New York Stock Exchange trading day on May 29, my brokers had purchased several tens of thousands of shares for my account. I hasten to emphasize that I bought the stocks for *investment* and not for speculation. I fully intend holding on to them, for I believe they will continue to increase in value over the years to come.

It has long been the custom for journalists and financial writers to interview successful businessmen and investors whenever there is an "unusual" stock market development. The opinions, information and advice gathered from these sources are then published, ostensibly for the guidance of less sophisticated investors. For as long as I can remember, veteran businessmen and investors—I among them—have been warning about the dangers of irrational stock speculation and hammering away at the theme that stock certificates are deeds of ownership in business enterprises and *not* betting slips.

Get-rich-quick schemes just don't work. If they did, then everyone on the face of the earth would be a millionaire. This holds as true for stock market dealings as it does for any other form of business activity.

Don't misunderstand me. It is possible to make money—and a great deal of money—in the stock market. But it can't be done overnight or by haphazard buying and selling. The big profits go to the intelligent, careful and patient investor, not to the reckless and overeager speculator. Conversely, it is the speculator who suffers the losses when the market takes a sudden downturn. The seasoned investor buys his stocks when they are priced low, holds them for the long-pull rise and takes in-between dips and slumps in his stride.

"Buy when stock prices are low—the lower the better—and hold onto your securities," a highly successful financier advised me years ago, when I first started buying stocks. "Bank on the trends and don't worry about the tremors. Keep your mind on the long-term cycles and ignore the sporadic ups and downs . . ."

Great numbers of people who purchase stocks seem unable to grasp these simple principles. They do not buy when prices are low. They are fearful of bargains. They wait until a stock goes by—and up—and then buy because they feel they are thus getting in on a sure thing. Very often, they buy too late—just before a stock has reached one of its peaks. Then they get caught and suffer losses when the price breaks even a few points.

Typical of these people is an acquaintance of mine with whom I had lunch one day in 1955. We talked about many things—including the stock market. During the course of the conversation I happened to mention that the X Corporation's shares were selling at 4½, and that I thought the stock would go up in price.

By late 1957, the stock stood at 11¼. I later learned that my acquaintance had kept his eye on the stock for two years and, when it reached 11¼, he finally decided it was safe to buy and purchased several hundred shares. He watched happily while the stock climbed to 13½ in the next six months. Then there was a dip. X shares fell to 10 and stayed there. My Johnny-come-lately acquaintance sold out and lost money. Those of us who'd bought early held on, for the securities were worth more than twice what we had paid for them.

Eventually, the stock rose again, going up several more points to reach another fairly steady price plateau. Today, it's around 15—and those of us who bought early are holding on to it firmly. I might add that we've also collected satisfactory dividends on the stock through the years.

I began buying common stocks at the depths of the Depression. Prices were at their lowest, and there weren't many stock buyers around. Most people with money to invest were unable to see the forest of potential profit for the multitudinous trees of their largely baseless fears. I had confidence in the future of the American economy and realized that the shares of many entirely sound companies with fine potentials were selling at only a fraction of their true worth.

When I first bought Tide Water Associated Oil Company stock in 1932, its price was as low as $2.12 per share. The average per-share open-market price of the stock rose steadily, as shown below:

1933	$ 8.23
1934	9.39
1935	11.61
1936	15.54
1937	20.83

The price fell off during the 1938 slump, but this was just one of the sporadic tremors. I not only held on to the shares I owned, but bought more.

My confidence was fully justified in the years that followed as the value of the stock increased many, many times, and I— along with all the other stockholders—also collected handsome dividends.

In May 1932, I also started purchasing Petroleum Corporation stock. In that month, I bought 10,000 shares at $3.45 per share. I continued to buy steadily until, by September 14, 1933, I held a total of 190,000 shares. In that month, the shares were worth nearly $15 each; the average per-share cost of my 190,000 shares was only $6.537.

I have reached back to the Depression era for two examples based on my own experiences. I could cite others from that period and from subsequent ones. Some stocks I own today are worth more than 100 times what I originally paid for them. But many other investors have had even greater successes. More examples would serve only to further underscore the same basic truth, one that every investor and would-be investor would do well to paste in his hat:

Sound stocks, purchased for investment when their prices are low and held for the long pull, are very likely to produce high profits through dividends and increases in value.

This is a self-evident "secret" of successful investment that vast numbers of people disregard. There are other not-so-secret secrets that investors would do well to learn and consider as inflexible rules in their stock market dealings.

Highly important among them is the axiom that no one should ever buy a stock without knowing as much as possible about the company that issues it. In more cases than legitimate brokers would care to count, such so-called investors have insisted on buying large numbers of shares in companies without having the foggiest notion of what those companies do or produce.

As I see it, the average person should consider the purchase of common stock as the investment of surplus capital for the purpose of earning an annual return on that capital and of eventually increasing the capital as much as possible.

The average individual begins "investing" by opening a savings account or by buying insurance or annuities. He usually graduates to buying Government bonds. Later, when he is more experienced and sure of himself, he may decide to invest in common stocks. If and when he does so, he should follow certain definite rules for his own protection and benefit.

In the main, the average investor should consider buying only such common stocks as are listed on a major stock exchange. There are many good reasons for this. Some unlisted stocks are worthless, bogus shares peddled by fly-by-night companies. Even when the unlisted stocks are legitimate the buyer often finds that he is "locked in" with his investment; it is frequently difficult to sell an unlisted security.

The person who buys or sells listed stocks can always be certain he is paying—or receiving—a price that is fair and bona fide to the extent that it has been set by buyers and sellers according to the law of supply and demand in a free market place. The same cannot always be said for unlisted stocks, which may be pegged at artificially high prices or, in some cases, have no value at all.

Common stocks should be purchased when their prices are low, not after they have risen to high levels during an upward bull-market spiral. Buy when everyone else is selling and hold on until everyone else is buying—this is more than just a catchy slogan. It is the very essence of successful investment.

History shows that the overall trend of stock prices—like the overall trend of living costs, wages and almost everything else—is up. Naturally there have been and always will be dips, slumps, recessions and even depressions, but these are invariably followed by recoveries which carry most stock prices to new highs. Assuming that a stock and the company behind it are sound, an investor can hardly lose if he buys shares at the bottom and holds them until the inevitable upward cycle gets well under way.

Withal, the wise investor realizes that it is no longer possible to consider the stock market as a whole. Today's stock market is far too vast and complex for anyone to make sweeping generalized predictions about the course the market as such will follow.

It is necessary to view the present-day stock market in terms of groups of stocks, but it is not enough merely to classify them as, say, industrials or aircrafts, and so on. This is an era of constant and revolutionary scientific and technological changes and advances. Not only individual firms, but also entire industries must be judged as to their ability to keep pace with the needs of the future. The investor has to be certain that neither the products of the company in which he invests nor the particular industry itself will become obsolete in a few years.

In the early part of the century, farsighted individuals realized that automobiles had more of a future than buckboards, that automobile-tire manufacturers' stocks were better investment bets than the stocks of firms that manufactured wagon wheels.

The trolley-car industry was a good bet—until trolley cars began to be supplanted by buses. Airplane makers who insisted on producing nothing but canvas-covered planes after the day of the all-metal airplane dawned had little future. Today, the manufacturer of jet or turboprop transport planes is much more likely to be in business and make money than one, say, who insisted on turning out trimotored, piston-engined transports.

It is indeed surprising that so many investors fail to recognize business situations only slightly less obvious than these dated or farfetched examples. They will buy stocks in faltering or dying firms and industries and ignore tempting opportunities to buy into companies and industries that cannot help but burgeon as time goes on.

It follows that the investor must know as much as he possibly can about the corporation in which he buys stock. The following are some of the questions for which he should get satisfactory answers before he invests his money:

1. What is the company's history: Is it a solid and reputable firm, and does it have able, efficient and seasoned management?

2. Is the company producing or dealing in goods or services for which there will be a continuing demand in the foreseeable future?

3. Is the company in a field that is not dangerously overcrowded, and is it in a good competitive position?

4. Are company policies and operations farsighted and aggressive without calling for unjustified and dangerous overexpansion?

5. Will the corporate balance sheet stand up under the close scrutiny of a critical and impartial auditor?

6. Does the corporation have a satisfactory earnings record?

7. Have reasonable dividends been paid regularly to stockholders? If dividend payments were missed, were there good and sufficient reasons?

8. Is the company well within safe limits insofar as both long- and short-term borrowing are concerned?

9. Has the price of the stock moved up and down over

the past few years without violently wide and apparently inexplicable fluctuations?

10. Does the per-share value of the company's net realizable assets exceed the stock exchange value of a common stock share at the time the investor contemplates buying?

Many stock buyers have failed to ask these questions. In some cases, they bought the stocks of companies that had not shown a profit for some time. But the issues would "get hot," as speculators are wont to say, and multiply several times over their issue price within a matter of weeks or even days. Then, someone would realize that the heat was being generated solely by irrational buying—and the prices would plummet.

I repeat that I personally believe that selected—and I want again to emphasize the word *selected*—common stocks are excellent investments. There are innumerable fine buys on the market today. Among them are many stocks issued by companies with net realizable assets two, three, four and even more times greater than the stock exchange value of their issued shares.

What does this mean to the investor? Well, for example, let's suppose that the mythical XYZ Corporation has realizable assets with a net value of $20,000,000. At the same time, it has 1,000,000 shares of common stock outstanding and the stock is selling at $10 per share. The arithmetic is simple. The $20,000,000 net value of the company's realizable assets is double the total $10,000,000 value of its outstanding common shares. Thus, anyone buying a share of the XYZ Corporation's common stock at $10 is buying $20 worth of actual, hard assets.

Such situations are not nearly so unusual as one might imagine—and the shrewd, seasoned investor takes the time and trouble to seek them out. Occasionally—though admittedly such instances are rare—especially astute investors discover companies that have undistributed surpluses equal to a sizable percentage of the market value of the outstanding common stock. Anyone buying stock in such a company is actually buying an amount of money equal to a goodly portion of his investment, as well as a share in the corporation's other assets.

I might point out, however, that the exact opposite may be

true, and that the investor will still be safe. An individual does not necessarily have to buy stocks in a company whose vaults are bulging with cash in order to make a sound investment. There are many times when an entirely healthy company will be very short of cash.

Another valuable investment secret is that the owners of sound securities should never panic and unload their holdings when prices skid. Countless individuals have panicked during slumps, selling out when their stocks fell a few points, only to find that before long the prices were once more rising.

The professional or experienced semiprofessional investor has little in common with speculators who hopefully play the market when prices are spiraling up. The veteran investor objectively looks for bargains in growth stocks—which he buys and holds, and from which he generally reaps handsome profits over a period of years. He banks on the climate—and makes all necessary allowances and takes all precautions so that he can ride out any stock market storms.

There is still a lingering misconception that the small or amateur investor is at the mercy of the big investors and the Wall Street financiers. This might have been the case in the dim, distant and unlamented days of Jay Gould, but nothing could be further from the truth today. No ruthless, rapacious Wall Street tycoon can rig the market or corner the stocks of an entire industry these days. For one thing, stock market transactions are closely regulated by such highly efficient and potent watchdog organizations and agencies as the Federal Securities and Exchange Commission—the SEC. For another, the common stocks of most large corporations are owned by thousands and tens of thousands of individuals, organizations, mutual fund groups and so on. "Big" investors seldom own more than a comparatively small percentage of a large corporation's common stock.

If anything, it is the professional investor who is at the mercy of the speculator and the amateur—at least in the sense that the latter categories of stock buyers and sellers set the pattern for the market.

The professional investor purchases stocks on what might be termed a scientific, or at least a cerebral, basis. He analyzes facts and figures objectively and with great care and does his buying for purposes of long-term investment. He is, in effect, banking that the stocks he buys will increase appreciably in value over the next few or several years.

It is the emotional nonprofessional investor who sends the price of a stock up or down in sharp, sporadic and more or less short-lived spurts. A politician's speech, an ivory-tower pundit's pronouncements or prophecies, a newspaper item or a whispered rumor—such things are enough to trigger wildly enthusiastic buying sprees or hysterical orgies of panicky selling by thousands of self-styled investors. The professional investor has no choice but to sit by quietly while the mob has its day, until the enthusiasm or the panic of the speculators and nonprofessionals have been spent.

The seasoned investor does not allow temporary fluctuations in stock-market prices to influence his decisions to any great extent. Usually, he waits until prices return to approximately the levels at which he wants to buy or sell. He is not impatient, nor is he even in a very great hurry, for he is an investor—not a gambler nor a speculator.

People often ask me what specific advice I would give to individuals who have various amounts—$1000, $10,000, $100,000 or even more—to invest in common stocks. My answers are always the same. Whether I had $100 or $1,000,-000 to invest, I would consider buying *only* such common stocks as are listed on a major stock exchange. I would apply the rules and tests I've enumerated and select the soundest and most promising growth stocks. And, I might add, I would certainly ignore the advice of promoters and theorists who peddle harebrained formulas or "secret" methods for making huge and quick profits on the stock market. There has been a spate of *How to Get Rich Overnight* books in recent years. Seasoned financiers and investors laugh at them—or rather, they feel only pity for the gullible individuals who follow the "advice" contained in such tomes. The May 1962 Wall Street collapse pulled down many of these "blinkered" speculators, so its history should be worth examining.

In order to achieve any understanding of that collapse, it is helpful to first quickly trace the course of the market over the preceding 12 years. The easiest way to do this is by following the Dow-Jones industrial average.

At the 1950 low, the Dow-Jones industrial average stood at 161.60. It climbed to 293.79 by the end of 1952, dropped to 255.49 in mid-1953, then climbed steadily to 521.04 in 1956, from which level it drifted down to around 420 at the end of 1957.

From 420 in 1957, the Dow-Jones average rose to well over 650 in 1959, made some up-and-down zigzags and hit a late-1960 low of 566.05. From that base, it shot up to a then all-time peak of 734.91 on December 13, 1961.

As the market moved upward through 1961, some Wall Street veterans dusted off the oft-quoted pre-1929 crash saying that the stock market was discounting not only the future, but the hereafter as well.

Many years ago, the per-share price *vs*. per-share earnings ratio was widely—though unofficially—adopted as a reliable rule-of-thumb indicator of stock values. "Ten times earnings" was long considered the maximum permissible price one could pay for a stock and still reasonably expect to make a profit.

Then, in the late 1920s, GM-Du Pont's John J. Raskob—whose outlook was judged quite bullish—ventured the opinion that certain stocks might be worth as much as 15 times their per-share earnings. After the 1929 crash, ratios were, of course, very much lower and, even as late as 1950, the price-earnings ratios of the stocks listed in the Dow-Jones industrial index averaged out to about 6:1.

Views on the price-earnings ratio underwent considerable revision in recent years. Some knowledgeable investors allowed that in a rapidly burgeoning economy, stocks of especially healthy companies might reasonably sell for as much as 20 times their per-share earnings. Other professional investors argued persuasively that when healthy companies had tangible assets with net, per-share replacement or liquidation values in excess of per-share prices, the importance of the price-earnings ratio would logically dwindle.

But few seasoned investors approved such situations as developed in 1960–1962, when frenzied buying drove prices so high that some issues were selling for more than 100 times their per-share earnings. In more than a few instances during the 1960–1962 period, staggering prices were paid for the stocks of companies that had only negligible assets, questionable potentials—and that hadn't shown much in the way of profits for a considerable time.

It has been suggested that the boom that began in 1960

was caused by people buying stocks as a hedge against inflation. If this is true, the insane inflation of certain common-stock prices was an extremely odd way to go about it. But the hedge theory appears even less valid when one remembers that buyers consistently ignored many fine stocks that, by any standards of measurement, were *under*priced and concentrated on certain issues, continuing to buy them after their prices had soared out of sight. All evidence inclines the observer to believe that the great mass of non-professional buyers was obeying a sort of herd instinct, following the crowd to snap up the popular issues without much regard for facts. Many people were doing their investment thinking—if it can properly be called that—with their emotions rather than with their heads. They looked for lightning-fast growth in stocks that were already priced higher than the limits of any genuine value levels to which they could conceivably grow in the foreseeable future.

It is an old Wall Street saw that the stock market will always find a reason for whatever it does—after having done it. Innumerable theories have been advanced to explain why the market broke on May 28, 1962. The blame has been placed on everything from "selling waves by foreign speculators" to the Kennedy Administration's reaction to the aborted steel industry price increase—in fact, on everything but the most obvious reasons.

The factors that bring on financial panics are many and varied. For example, in 1869, the cause was an attempted corner on gold. In 1873 and 1907, bank failures started the trouble. In 1929, the stock market was vastly overpriced, and the general state of American business and the rate of America's economic expansion were such as to justify little or none of the stock buying that carried prices to the towering peaks from which they inevitably had to fall.

Despite all the efforts that have been expended to draw a close parallel between the 1929 crash and the 1962 price break, the two have practically nothing in common.

True, some segments of the stock market were grossly overpriced in 1960–1962; far too many stocks were priced far too high. But the nation's business outlook was generally good in 1962, and the economy was expanding at a merry clip. There were no hidden, deep-down structural flaws in the economy such as there had been in 1929.

There were other great differences. In 1929, stock speculation was done mainly on borrowed money; shares were purchased on the most slender of margins. Thus, when prices collapsed, credit collapsed, too.

Then, of course, there is the most important difference of all, the one the calamity howlers conveniently forgot. May 28, 1962, was not a crash. It was an adjustment—albeit a somewhat violent one.

As I've said, some stocks were selling for more than 100 times their earnings during the height of the 1960–1962 boom. Now, it would be rather difficult for a company to expand enough to justify stock prices that were 100 times the company's per-share earnings. Even assuming that every penny of the company's earnings were paid out in dividends to common-stockholders, the stockholders would still be receiving only a one-percent return on their investment. But if all earnings were distributed in dividends, there would be no money left for the company to spend on expansion. That, of course, would effectively eliminate any possibility of capital growth. Yet, even with these glaringly self-evident truths staring them in the face, people bought overpriced stocks.

Such were the difficult situations that developed—and that caused the stock market to fall. Experienced investors should have been able to read the warning signals loud and clear long before the May 28 break took place.

As I stated previously, the Dow-Jones industrial average shot to its all-time high of 734.91 on December 13, 1961. The downward movement began immediately afterward and continued through December 1961 and January 1962. There was a brief recovery that continued until March, when the Dow-Jones average edged up over 720, but the graph line shows the recovery was an uncertain, faltering one. The downward trend was resumed in March—and the graph line from then on makes a steep descent that is broken by only a few spasmodic upward jogs.

The May 28, 1962, price break had its beginnings in December 1961. The downward adjustment was evidently needed and unavoidable. That it culminated in the sharp price plunge of May 28 was due to the emotional reaction

—verging on panic—shown by inexperienced investors who were unable to realize that what was happening *had* to happen and, what was worse, who understood almost nothing of what was going on around them. To paraphrase Abraham Lincoln, *all* stock market investors cannot fool themselves *all* of the time. The awakening had to come—and it did.

The anatomy of a stock market boom-and-bust such as the country experienced in 1962 is not too difficult to analyze. The seeds of any bust are inherent in any boom that outstrips the pace of whatever solid factors gave it its impetus in the first place.

An old and rather corny comedy line has it that the only part of an automobile that cannot be made foolproof by a safety device is the nut that holds the wheel. By much the same token, there are no safeguards that can protect the emotional investor from himself.

Having bid the market up irrationally, these emotional investors became terrified and unloaded their holdings just as irrationally. Unfortunately, an emotionally inspired selling wave snowballs and carries with it the prices of all issues, even those that should be going up rather than down.

Withal, I believe it is absolutely essential for the American public to bear in mind that:

1. The nation's economy was relatively sound on Friday afternoon, May 25, 1962, when the New York Stock Exchange closed for the weekend.

2. The U.S. economy was just as sound on the following Monday morning, when the stock exchange reopened.

3. The economy was basically no less sound when trading ended on that hectic Monday. Few—if any—industrial orders were canceled. Few—if any—jobs were lost. Few—if any— business establishments were forced to close their doors. Few —if any—investors, large or small, were completely wiped out as so many had been in 1929.

I realize that all this is scant comfort to those who lost money when stock prices fell on May 28. It can only be hoped that they will profit from the painful lesson.

The wise investor will recognize that many stocks being offered on the market are still considerably *under*priced. For example, there are many issues selling for as little as one-third or even one-fourth the net, per-share liquidation values of the issuing company's assets. To understand what this can mean to the stockholder, consider the case of the Honolulu Oil Company.

A few years ago, the directors and stockholders of the Honolulu Oil Company decided for reasons of their own to dissolve the company. One company in which I hold a substantial interest and another oil company learned of this decision and together signified their desire to buy Honolulu Oil's assets.

The stockholders of Honolulu Oil had their choice of two ways in which they could sell their company's assets. First, they could sell their stock to the two buying companies. Or, alternatively, they could hold their stock, sell the actual assets and distribute the proceeds among themselves before formally dissolving their company.

Honolulu Oil's shareholders chose the latter method. The company's stock was selling at around $30 per share—but, so valuable were its tangible assets, that the price the buying companies paid for them worked out to about $100 per share. This, of course, was the sum each Honolulu stockholder received for each share he held when the company was dissolved. In other words, the cash value of Honolulu Oil's assets was more than three times as much as the total value of its issued stock.

Naturally, shareholders can reap this particular type of windfall profit only when the company concerned is dissolved. But it should be plain to see how much added safety there is in investing in a company that has tangible assets with a net liquidation value greater than the value of its stock. If, as an example, the net liquidation value is three times that of the stock, then, in effect, each dollar of the stockholder's investment is secured by three dollars' worth of realizable assets.

There are more such companies than one might imagine. They can be found in various industries, but I am most familiar with companies in the petroleum industry and, more particularly, with those engaged in the business of producing oil.

Several oil stocks issued by sound, thriving companies are selling at prices well within any reasonable price-earnings ratio limits. Some of these oil companies also have tangible assets worth three, four and even more times the total value of their issued stock. It might be of interest to consider just one reason why this is so. Producing oil companies normally carry their oil and gas leases at cost on their balance sheets. A lease for which a company paid, say, $25,000 is carried at that figure even though it covers a property on which the proven crude-oil reserves in place are, as is entirely possible, 50,000,-000 barrels. On the books, the lease is shown as an asset worth $25,000, even though any other producing oil company would gladly pay several million dollars to take it over. The implications of this bit of accounting intelligence will not be lost on the alert investor. Similar situations exist in many other industries, and the astute investor will find them and profit from them.

My own confidence in the stock market has not been shaken by the May 28 price break nor by later drops. I am still a heavy investor in common stocks. I'm still banking—to the tune of many millions of dollars—on the healthy climate of the American economy and the bright future of American business.

This, in essence, is the only advice and counsel a successful, experienced investor can give to anyone who wishes to reap the benefits of a boom and to avoid the losses of a bust.

A
REAL APPROACH
TO REAL ESTATE

Almost every American family has its tales of fabulous real estate opportunities that were missed or ignored by one or another of its members at some time in the past.

"Forty years ago, my grandfather turned down a chance to buy 1000 acres of land at $10 per acre. Today, that land is worth $30,000 an acre . . ."

"I could have bought an empty lot at the south end of Main Street for $750 in 1932. Last week, that same lot sold for $20,000 . . ."

"We sold our house for $5000 just before World War Two. Now the land on which the house stood is alone worth more than ten times that amount . . ."

Such stories are to be heard whenever real estate crops up as a subject for discussion. I have more than a few to tell about my own family—and about myself.

In the 1880s, the city of Detroit, Michigan, had a population of about 116,000. My mother's brother-in-law, Travers Leach, owned a 160-acre farm outside what were then Detroit's city limits. Sometime before the turn of the century, Leach sold the farm for a few thousand dollars, making what he considered a fair profit on the sale.

Unfortunately, Travers Leach could not foresee that by 1920 the population of Detroit would soar to nearly 1,000,000 and that a mushrooming urban area would engulf his farmland. Had he held onto his farm, he and his heirs would have become multimillionaires. By 1920, each of his 160 acres was worth many, many times what the entire property had been worth in the 1890s. Today, of course, a 160-acre tract in what has become virtually the heart of Detroit would fetch an astronomical sum.

A Real Approach to Real Estate

In 1906, my father could have purchased all of 70-square-mile Santa Catalina Island off the Southern California coast for only $250,000. He turned the offer down. Catalina Island was later purchased by the Wrigley interests and transformed into one of the best-known and most profitable resort areas on the West Coast. For years, the value of Santa Catalina Island has been calculated in the tens of millions of dollars.

During the Depression years, I could have picked up huge parcels of undeveloped land in Southern California and elsewhere for only a few dollars per acre. In those days, the tracts were far outside the limits of any incorporated town or city. Since 1945, the towns and cities have grown with lightning speed, spreading out in all directions. The once practically worthless tracts have become thriving residential or industrial areas. Much land that sold for as little as $500 an acre—and even less—in the Depression days now brings $50,000 and even more per acre.

But, for every such story of missed opportunity, there is one that tells of opportunities which were recognized and exploited to the full. It is obvious that someone ultimately reaped huge profits from Travers Leach's Detroit farmland. The Wrigley interests recognized the potentials of Catalina Island, bought it and profited accordingly. Other men purchased the tracts I turned down in the 1930s and eventually reaped gigantic profits by subdividing and developing the property.

My father may have bobbled his chance to buy Catalina Island at a bargain price, but he made many other shrewd and profitable real estate investments. In 1907, Father bought some land on Wilshire Boulevard in Los Angeles for about $10,000 and built our family home on it. The land was then well outside the city's built-up areas—so much so that it was surrounded on all sides by meadowland, and the nearest paved road was more than a mile distant. In the 1920s, he was offered $300,000 for the property, but he refused to sell. The property, which is still owned by "Getty interests," is now worth somewhere in the neighborhood of $2,000,000.

I, myself, have bought real estate at rock-bottom prices and have seen the values of the properties increase in my own lifetime—often even within a few years. On one occasion some years ago, for example, I purchased several dozen acres of land in Malibu, California, paying about $150,000 for the property. Today, real estate brokers tell me, I could probably realize $4,000,000 on my investment if I were to subdivide and sell the land.

I'm seldom eager to sell simply for the sake of making a quick profit. I always remember the lease I bought for $8000 from a friend who was doubling his money overnight.

Later, I drilled four oil wells on that property and, in the next 12 years, those four wells showed an excess recovery—a net profit—of $800,000.

I have not cited these examples of my successful real estate dealings in order to boast or gloat. I mentioned them solely to show that real estate *can* be a highly profitable form of investment.

At first glance, it might seem that I consider it easy to make money in real estate. I probably appear to be expounding a theory that one needs only to buy cheap land far outside a city's expanding limits and then wait until the city grows out to meet the property, and that the buyer will make money if he can hold onto his property long enough.

Unfortunately, it's seldom as simple as that. The real estate investor can never be certain that cities will mushroom in any particular direction, nor even that they will grow at all. If he buys property within the city, called income property, he has no assurance that it will increase in value. It may, in fact, lose value if, for example, a neighborhood ceases to be fashionable.

Then, no matter how low the price of an undeveloped property may be, its purchase still entails a capital outlay—and the capital sum may have to be tied up for a very long time without producing any income before property values begin to rise. Also, there are property taxes, assessments and other expenses which must be paid, and these can add up to large sums over the years.

Some time ago, a friend of mine bought 200 undeveloped acres at the northern edge of a Midwestern city, paying $100,000 for the land. He was quite correct in his basic assumption that the city would expand and grow—but he could not foresee that when it did, public taste and preference would cause the growth to take place in the city's southern and eastern sections.

My friend still owns the property, which is worth no more today than it was when he bought it. His $100,000 investment has brought him absolutely no income for more than a decade, and it has been necessary for him to pay annual property taxes on the acreage. In addition, he has spent sizable amounts in efforts to attract buyers for the property—all to no avail. He has already suffered considerable financial loss. He will continue to lose money on his investment unless he can sell the land, for there is no indication that the city's northern suburbs will ever find favor with homeowners or industrial firms.

In short, a prospective investor must always bear in mind that while real estate can be a highly profitable form of investment, it can also prove quite risky. Often there are many variable factors which affect the value of a property, and these factors are not always obvious even to experienced eyes. It is sometimes difficult to appraise the value of a given property accurately, and mistakes in appraisal can be costly. Another potential drawback to investing heavily in real estate is that an individual who ties a large amount of his capital up in real property and then has a sudden need for cash may well find it difficult to sell and realize cash quickly without incurring considerable losses.

In real estate, as in the stock market, it is the intelligent, patient investor who is most likely to make money in the long run. The real estate speculator, like his stock market counterpart, may make some short-term profits, but he takes much greater chances and his profits will never be anywhere near those of the investor.

There are two kinds of real estate investors. The first includes those who buy at very low prices before an upward trend begins and hold onto their properties for many years, patiently waiting for values to rise to high levels. They may buy undeveloped land with, possibly, a view to subdividing it, or they may purchase income property which they hope will eventually increase in value, even while it produces regular returns on their invested capital. The second type of real estate investor buys soon after a real estate boom has already begun. He pays more for a property than investors in the first category because prices are already on the way up when he gets into the market. On the other hand, he immobilizes his capital for much shorter periods.

Naturally, everyone would like to be the first kind of investor. The trouble is that not too many people have large amounts of capital they can invest and allow to lie more or less fallow for long periods. Also, there aren't many people who can foresee a boom early enough or gauge its duration with sufficient accuracy to take advantage of it.

One man I know correctly anticipated the post-War housing shortage and bought several large apartment houses at comparatively low prices in 1943. In 1950, he was offered 80 percent more than he had paid for the properties.

"I'm going to sell out," he announced to his real estate broker. "I've made a fairly good income on my investment over the last seven years, but I figure I had best take my profit now. I don't believe that property values can possibly go any higher than they are."

"I think you're making a big mistake," the broker cautioned. "If I were you, I'd hold on. Property values will go considerably higher in the next few years. You're going to miss a wonderful opportunity if you sell."

The man ignored his broker's prophetic advice and sold his apartment houses in 1950. He has been regretting his decision ever since. Today, the properties are worth at least three times what he paid for them in 1943.

Many investors have made the same error during the current real estate boom. They sold out prematurely because they were convinced the peak had been reached or that it would be reached within a very short time. They feared the consequences of the bust they were certain would follow. Their reasoning and their fears were based on past experiences or on recollections of the histories of such ill-starred real estate booms as those which drove real property prices into the stratosphere in Florida, California and elsewhere in the 1920s.

I, personally, do not believe there is any similarity between those booms and the one which began at the end of World War Two and is still continuing today. The great real estate balloons which were inflated—and then burst so disastrously

—during the Roaring Twenties were almost entirely fueled by purely speculative buying and selling. Despite all the frenzied activity of property trading, there was little genuine desire for ownership on the part of the speculators. In those days, a piece of property could—and often did—change hands dozens of times, but not because anyone anywhere along the line actually wanted to own land, build a home or operate income property. Each momentary "owner" of a piece of property had but a single thought in his mind—to sell as soon as he could and to make as large a profit as possible.

For example, there were an estimated 2000 real estate offices and 25,000 real estate salesmen in Miami, Florida, alone in 1925. Theoretically, they sold property—ranging from single lots to huge tracts of land. In actual practice, all that most of them sold were "binders." The buyer paid a small percentage of the agreed sales price of a property and received a receipt which constituted a binder; the property was then his until the next payment fell due 30 or 60 days later. The overwhelming majority of buyers sold their binders just as soon as they could realize a profit on them. With prices spiraling wildly, they seldom had to wait more than a few days—or at most, a few weeks—before finding another feverish speculator who would give them more money than they'd paid.

There was more truth than humor in the following tale that made the rounds at the height of the 1920s' Florida land boom. According to the story, a Miami realtor had taken a prospective buyer out to look at a dismal and utterly useless swamp tract. The client stared at the forbidding landscape in dismay.

"No one could ever build anything on this land!" he said. "It's worthless!"

"So what?" the realtor shrugged. "Land down here ain't for ownin'; it's for tradin' . . . !"

The post-World War Two real estate boom is entirely different from those which took place during the Twenties. There is a solid demand for building sites, for homes, commercial and industrial sites and buildings and income properties. The people and the firms who are in the market for such properties are serious buyers. They want to buy or build houses, stores, factories—or whatever—for their own use or for the purpose of leasing or renting them to others in order to earn income for themselves. In short, they really want to *own* the properties they buy. The number of out-and-out speculators today is, as far as I can see, negligible.

Current real estate prices aren't high because they have been driven up by irresponsible speculation, as was so often the case in the past. Prices have risen because a constantly increasing population with money to invest has created—and continues to create—a great demand for real property of all kinds in almost every part of the country.

I, for one, do not anticipate any major break in real estate values in the foreseeable future. Some soft spots may develop here and there and there may be tendencies to oversell or overbuild in some areas, but I believe the over-all trend in real estate will continue to be up for a considerable time to come.

Of late, the companies in which I hold substantial interests have made sizable investments in real estate. The Tidewater Oil Company Building on Wilshire Boulevard in Los Angeles was completed not long ago at a cost of nearly $10,000,000. This building is designed for expansion after restrictive zoning regulations now in force have expired. The new 15-story Skelly Oil Company Building in Tulsa, Oklahoma, also represents a $10,000,000 investment. The even newer 22-story Getty Oil Company Building in New York City involved an investment of some $14,000,000.

I would imagine that the real estate investments these companies and I have undertaken in recent years provide convincing demonstrations of the confidence my associates and I have in the reality of real estate values.

Investors can find many potentially profitable opportunities in real estate today. They must, however, know what they are doing before and after they invest their money if they hope to reap profits. I think that I've already indicated that real estate is not always the safest form of investment for the inexperienced. This applies even to the most common type of real estate investment—home buying or building.

The home builder or buyer should take great care in selecting the site or house he buys. He should, for example, acquaint himself thoroughly with the zoning regulations which govern building and the use of property in the neighborhood or section in which the property he wishes to buy is located. It's not enough merely to ask the real estate salesman or the neighbors. Many a happy family has moved into its vine-covered dream cottage only to wake up one fine morning and discover that a glue factory or sewage-disposal plant was being built next door.

The home builder or buyer should also know something —and the more the better—about building. He should be able to judge—at least within reasonable limits—whether or not a house is built well. If he doesn't know about such things himself, he should most certainly have someone who *does* know make an inspection of the house for him before he buys, or keep an eye on the progress of construction if he builds.

As for the professional or semiprofessional real estate investor, in order to have any hope of success, he must have knowledge of a vast range of subjects running the alphabetical gamut from architecture to zoning laws. He should also retain a much-better-than-average lawyer. If it's true that possession is nine points of the law, it's equally true that nine tenths of the problems involved in the possession of real property are legal ones.

It's not possible to list any specific, universally applicable rules to guide the real estate investor. There are far too many different types of real property—ranging from single lots in uninhabited areas to entire complexes of residential, industrial or commercial buildings. The rules investors follow—or should follow—vary widely according to the type of property involved, the use which is to be made of it and local and even individual considerations. Nonetheless, there *are* some general rules and pointers which provide a valuable checklist of things to do—and not to do—for anyone who is thinking of making an investment in any kind of real estate.

1. Make a thorough study of the real estate market and its prospects in your area before you buy. Naturally, you should seek to buy when prices are low and the indications are that values will rise. Always take into consideration such factors as the rate of population increase and the general prospects of business in the area. There is no quicker way to lose money in real estate than by investing it in property located in declining areas.

2. Know or learn as much as possible about every aspect

of the particular use to which you intend putting the property you wish to buy. In other words, don't buy a house unless you're certain that it's suited to the requirements of your family and that it's well built. Don't plan on having a house built unless you know something about building—or at the very least until you've found an architect and a building contractor in whom you have complete confidence.

Don't consider buying, say, a motel unless you know enough about motel management to have a fair chance of operating it profitably—or again at the very least, until you know enough to efficiently supervise anyone you hire to run the motel for you.

3. Deal only through licensed and reputable real estate brokers. Beware the fast-talking, high-pressure real estate salesman who promises everything—verbally. He is probably a fly-by-night who doesn't much care what he sells you or anyone else.

4. If you buy a property with a view to improving it or building on it, be certain that you have adequate capital or are able to obtain adequate financing to complete the project.

5. If at all possible, always obtain at least one impartial, third-party appraisal of any property before you buy it.

6. If buying a building of any kind—be it a Cape Cod cottage, 1000-room hotel or Willow Run-size factory—have it inspected carefully by qualified and disinterested architects or builders before entering into any building commitments. If buying an existing income property such as an apartment house, have the owner's books checked by a disinterested accountant. If the owner of the building or the income property balks at such inspections, look out.

7. Whether you're in the market for a cabin site or a skyscraper, shop around widely and cautiously. Unless you happen to run across an irresistible bargain you must snap up immediately, take your time about making up your mind. Don't allow yourself to be stampeded into paying any deposits or binders until you're absolutely certain you've found the property you want. Remember that the purchase of real property usually involves heavy capital investment; don't take unnecessary chances with your money.

8. Make certain you have the best available legal advice

before signing any agreements, contracts or other documents. I do not mean to suggest that there is anything dishonest or misleading in the majority of such documents. On the other hand, few laymen are able to follow the labyrinthine mazes of legal terminology which are used in them. To avoid misunderstandings, it is always best to have an attorney translate the "whereas"-studded fine-print clauses into coherent everyday English. Even seasoned real estate investors sometimes fail to have this done—and the ensuing squabbles between buyers and sellers usually wind up in courtrooms.

9. Always insure the title to any property you buy. Even the most meticulous title search may fail to turn up all the pertinent facts about the history of a property. The cost of title insurance is negligible. The expense of fighting a lawsuit over a clouded title can be staggering—as many real estate investors, I among them, have discovered to their regret.

10. Once you've bought your property, treat it as a long-term investment, not as a short-term speculation. You'll find that—99 times out of a hundred—you'll make much greater profits that way. In fact, if you wish to make money in real estate, always think in terms of investing and never in terms of speculating.

These ten pointers do not, by any means, comprise an all-inclusive guide to successful real estate investment. Nor does the individual who follows them—however faithfully—have any guarantee that he will make a profit when he invests his money in real property.

But, I believe that the person who observes these rules goes a long way toward eliminating a significant portion of the most common dangers inherent in any transaction involving real property. And that, in itself, is sufficient to give him a head start on the road to successful real estate investment.

FINE ART:
THE FINEST
INVESTMENT

Newspaper editors seldom allot front-page space to art—
and more's the pity. But art made headlines throughout
the world not long ago, when the great Erickson collection
of old masters was sold at auction in New York City. Among
the 24 paintings that had been collected by the late advertising magnate Alfred W. Erickson and that had been ordered
sold by the executors of his widow's estate, were: one major
and two lesser Rembrandts, a Fragonard, a Crivelli and works
by Holbein the Younger, Vandyke, Cranach the Elder and
Terborch.

The major Rembrandt, *Aristotle Contemplating the Bust
of Homer,* and Fragonard's *La Liseuse* were exceptionally
choice items over which any collector's or museum curator's
mouth would water. It was generally conceded that the
paintings would fetch record prices and for weeks before
the sale the entire art world buzzed with speculation about
the sums likely to be involved and who the highest bidders
would be. Top presale estimates were $1,800,000 for the
Rembrandt and $350,000 for the Fragonard.

Actually, the amounts bid and paid at the auction were
far greater than those predicted by even the most educated
estimators. *Aristotle Contemplating the Bust of Homer,* the
only important Rembrandt not then in a museum, was purchased by New York's Metropolitan Museum of Art, which
paid a resounding $2,300,000 for it. This price was much the
highest ever paid for a single painting, twice the previous
record $1,166,400 Andrew Mellon paid the Soviet Govern-
ment in 1931 to get Raphael's *Alba Madonna* out of the
U.S.S.R. and into the National Gallery in Washington.

Fragonard's *La Liseuse* brought $875,000 and was purchased for the National Gallery. This represented the second highest price paid for a picture at an art auction since 1959, when Rubens' *Adoration of the Magi* was sold for $770,000. Incidentally, I attended that sale, going to $560,000 before dropping out of the bidding.

The point of all this is simply that the art market is booming and that fine art is a fine—and possibly the finest—investment in more ways than one. But then, art has long been a fine investment.

Alfred Erickson purchased *Aristotle Contemplating the Bust of Homer* from Duveen Brothers in 1928, when he paid $750,000 for it. During the depths of the Depression, he sold it back to the Duveens for $500,000 and then, in 1936, bought it again for $590,000. Simple arithmetic shows that he paid a total of $840,000 for the picture—and that the difference between this over-all purchase price and the most recent sale price is $1,460,000.

True, on the face of it, it appears that Erickson took a one-third loss between the time he first bought the painting and sold it back to Duveens'. But this must be viewed in light of the general economic conditions prevailing at the respective times involved. Alfred Erickson first bought in 1928, a peak-prosperity year. He sold when the Depression was approaching its lowest lows.

To obtain a proper perspective, it is necessary to remember what happened to business and all forms of investment during corresponding periods. Stocks plummeted, even such bluest of blue chips as U.S. Steel, which fell from a peak 261¾ to 21¼. In 1932, U.S. Industry was operating at well below 50 percent of the maximum levels it had reached before the 1929 crash. Wages paid out in 1932 were 60 percent less than in 1929; dividends paid by companies still able to pay dividends were 57 percent less. Considered against this background, Erickson's temporary 33⅓-percent loss on his painting would seem strong verification, indeed, of my contention that art *is* a fine investment.

Don't misunderstand me. Being a collector myself, I would be the last person in the world to suggest that Alfred W. Erickson bought—or that any serious collector buys—works of art for the purpose of realizing a financial profit on their subsequent sale. I'm only too well aware that art collectors are just that, and not art dealers.

Aline B. Saarinen, analyzing the motives of great American art collectors, writes: "Their overpowering common denominator is this: For each of them, the collecting of art was a primary means of expression."

Jacques Lipchitz, the sculptor, who owns one of the world's finest collections of primitive art, says, "Collecting is for learning about the human being and the way he feels and expresses himself, and about the material he uses to express himself and the way he uses the material."

I find nothing exceptionable in these opinions, but my own views go a step or two further. Like most serious collectors, I by no means consider the works of art I own as inanimate ornamental possessions. To me, they are vital embodiments of their creators. They mirror the hopes and frustrations of those who created them—and the times and places in which they were created. Although the artists may be long dead, and even the civilizations in which they worked long since disintegrated, their art lives on.

The interest and pleasure an individual takes in his collection does not stem from the monetary value of the works of art he owns. They derive from the enduring beauty of the art and from a realization of the validity and permanence of the fundamental values that art represents. The collector takes pleasure in the beauty of art, and he never really ceases to be stimulated by it.

The 16th Century Italian poet Federico da Porto admitted he was "stupefied and overwhelmed" by what he saw when he visited the magnificent collection of the Venetian statesman-historian Marino Sanudo. Da Porto's poem marking the visit indicates that collectors of the 1500s were no different from those of today—and that he, himself, was infected by the sense of exhilaration and gratification that Sanudo obviously possessed in no less measure than do his modern-day collector counterparts. Wrote Da Porto:

> *Then up the stairs you lead us, and we find*
> *A spacious corridor before us spread,*
> *As if it were another ocean full*
> *Of rarest things; the wall invisible*

Fine Art: The Finest Investment

With glorious pictures hid—no blank appears,
But various figures, men of every guise;
A thousand unaccustomed scenes we see.
Here Spain, there Greece, and here the apparel fair
Of France.

It is of such stuff that collections—and collectors—are made. The collector marvels at the wonders of the art he owns —and he displays his possessions proudly, sharing their beauty with others. Certainly, his principal concern is not with the pecuniary value of his works of art—although collectors will often stretch and even wreck their budgets to obtain an object they desire.

Nonetheless, it remains an undeniable fact that fine art is a fine investment. The dollars-and-cents values of paintings, sculpture, tapestries, fine antique furniture and virtually all forms of art have shown a marked tendency to rise—and even soar—over the years. Much of this, of course, is due to the increased—and still increasing—awareness that art represents basic values that are not only lasting, but that become more valid as time goes on. Thus, there is competition to secure works of art—and thus their monetary value, the price people are willing to pay for them, rises.

The trend has not been limited to art of any particular school, style, period or medium. A few examples taken at random should suffice to illustrate the manner in which the money values of art have spiraled.

In 1885, the Victoria and Albert Museum of London bought more than 1000 drawings by the 18th Century Italian master Giovanni Battista Tiepolo. Although Tiepolo's breathtaking frescos adorned the Labia Palace in Venice, the Kaisersaal of the Prince-Bishop's House in Würzburg, Germany, the throne room of Spain's King Charles III and dozens of other great homes, churches and public buildings, his drawings were not then in vogue. The Victoria and Albert Museum paid about ten cents apiece for them. Today, *each drawing* would bring at least $1500—if the museum wanted to sell them, which, of course, it has no intention of doing.

The 19th Century English master Joseph M. W. Turner produced many fine water-color paintings during his long and successful career. In the 1940s, these sold for between $500 and $1000 apiece. At the present time, a large Turner water color will fetch anywhere up to $25,000.

Paul Gauguin's *Te Tiai Nei Au I Te Rata*—"I Await the Letter"—is said to have once sold for less than $50. At an auction in 1959, the painting realized more than $300,000. In that same year, one of Braque's early works—which had once been sold at auction for $15—was eagerly snapped up by the Queensland Art Gallery at a price of $155,000. Also in 1959, an illuminated manuscript prepared under the direction of Matthew Paris at St. Albans Abbey about 1250 A.D. sold for $190,000—as against the $115,000 paid for a comparable manuscript not very long before.

Such a list could be extended almost indefinitely and expanded to include practically every medium, period and school of art, from prehistoric figurines to contemporary works by abstract expressionists, action painters and representatives of the welding-torch school of sculpture—and most certainly such things as tapestries, carpets and fine antique furniture.

I have seen the money value of the works of art I've purchased increase and even multiply several times during the years since I acquired them.

In 1938, I purchased the historic and almost legendary Ardabil Persian carpet, which had been made on the royal looms of Tabriz in 1535. Moslem Persians had considered this fabulous, 11-by-24-foot carpet so beautiful that they had said it was "too good for Christian eyes to gaze upon." But "Christian eyes" had often "gazed upon" the Ardabil carpet and had marveled at what they saw.

"It is worth all the pictures ever painted," the American artist James Whistler declared after seeing the Ardabil. The carpet, a symphony of glowing colors executed with unsurpassed artistry and fantastic in its detail, is generally acknowledged tó be one of the two finest carpets in the Western world.

The Ardabil sold for $27,000 in 1910. Nine years later, it was purchased by the famous art expert–dealer Lord Duveen, who paid $57,000 for it. I bought the carpet from Lord Duveen in 1938, paying him $68,000. I subsequently received many offers for the Ardabil, including one of $250,000 from Egypt's then-King Farouk. I declined his offer along with all the others. In 1958, the Los Angeles County Museum

—to which I had donated the carpet—placed its value at $1,000,000, almost 40 times the price for which it had been sold in 1910 and nearly 15 times what I had paid for it.

In the same year that I bought the Ardabil carpet, I also acquired the fine Rembrandt portrait of Marten Looten, which the great Dutch master had painted in 1632. I paid $65,000 for the picture and considered it a bargain, for I had been quite prepared to go as high as $100,000 to obtain it. The market value of the painting increased fantastically through the years. How much it would fetch at a sale today is a purely academic question, for the portrait was also donated to the Los Angeles County Museum. However, the record $2,300,000 paid for Rembrandt's *Aristotle Contemplating the Bust of Homer* would seem to indicate that *Marten Looten* would bring a price many times greater than what I paid for it.*

But one does not have to buy the works of acknowledged old masters to obtain fine works of art—or, for that matter, to make excellent investments.

For example, the Spanish artist Joaquín Sorolla y Bastida lived from 1893 to 1923. In 1933, I attended an art sale in New York City, saw some of his work and thought it excellent. I bought ten of Sorolla y Bastida's paintings for a total of well under $10,000. By 1938, the world had begun to really appreciate the artist's talent, and the ten paintings had risen in value to a total of $40,000. Today Joaquín Sorolla y Bastida is ranked among the top 20 Spanish painters of all time—and I hesitate to guess what the ten paintings I bought in 1933 would bring if placed on sale.

---

* In addition to the million-dollar Ardabil carpet and Rembrandt's *Marten Looten,* J. Paul Getty has donated other extremely valuable pieces of fine art to the Los Angeles County Museum. Incidentally, he derived no tax benefits for himself by making the gifts to the institution.

He still has a multimillion-dollar collection, but even a large part of this has been donated to the J. Paul Getty Museum. The collection includes Boucher tapestries, rare carpets and a collection of French 18th Century furniture which Sir James Mann, director of the Wallace Collection and an outstanding authority on the subject, has judged to be finer than the one owned by the Louvre. There are also Fourth and Fifth Century, B.C., Greek marbles—including some of the famed Elgin marbles—terra cottas, bronzes, Roman portraits and sculpture and the renowned Lansdowne *Hercules.* Among the paintings are works by Titian, Lotto, Tintoretto, Rubens, Gainsborough and other masters. All the items are sumptuously housed and displayed in Getty's own magnificent Ranch-Museum on the Pacific Coast Highway in Malibu, California. The museum is open to the public without charge. *Editor*

Nor is it even necessary to spend thousands—or even many hundreds—of dollars to start and build an art collection that will almost certainly increase in value in the years to come. There are—and always have been—many opportunities to obtain real bargains in art.

I might add that, in some remote corner of every art collector's heart, there always lurks a secret hope of making a discovery, of picking up a painting at a bargain price and then learning it is really the long-lost work of some great master. This does happen on occasion. I know, for it happened to me.

About 25 years ago, I attended an art sale at Sotheby's in London. Among the objects on sale was a rather battered Italian painting of a madonna—a work, the Sotheby experts declared, produced by some unknown artist. Although the madonna was badly begrimed and in a poor state of preservation, I liked the picture; it was, I thought, reminiscent of Raphael. I bought it—for $200.

In 1963, I decided to have the painting cleaned. The job was entrusted to the famous firm of restorers, Thomas Agnew & Sons. Representatives of the firm soon called me excitedly. The painting was, indeed, the work of Raphael, they said— and this was quickly authenticated by such leading art experts as Alfred Scharf. The painting I purchased for $200 has proved to be Raphael's *Madonna di Loreto,* painted in 1508–1509. Its real value: upwards of a million dollars.

I'll grant there isn't much likelihood that the average art buyer will pick up a $300,000 Gauguin, a $155,000 Braque or even a $1500 Tiepolo for pennies in a corner junk shop. On the other hand, such remarkable finds as a London art critic's recent discovery in a Dublin shed of five soot-blackened canvases which proved to be important Guardi figure compositions serve to keep all art buyers' hopes high.

Certainly, it is often possible to buy good, reasonably priced works by lesser artists, particularly in out-of-the-way art stores, antique shops, and even second-hand bookstores, which are frequently excellent places to pick up prints and etchings. Then, of course, one can shop very advantageously for the works of talented young artists who have not yet arrived, but who show promise. It should hardly be necessary to point out that an artist does not yet have to be established for his work to be good and have lasting value.

Even people with very slender budgets can acquire works of art that will prove excellent investments in beauty, pleasure —and also in the financial sense. I know many individuals who have paid modest prices for works of art and have then seen the market value of their purchases spiral upward.

The experiences of a journalist friend of mine provide a trenchant four-in-one example of what an individual with a little common sense and taste can do. This journalist travels extensively to New York, London, Paris and Venice. By no means an art expert and far from rich, he likes to browse— and occasionally buy—in art, antique and secondhand bookstores. His tastes run quite a gamut; he buys things that please him and satisfy him aesthetically, regardless of whether they are ancient or ultramodern. But he shops carefully—and the collection for which he paid about $2000 over the last six years already has a market value of at least $8000.

Typical of his successful investments are these four purchases, each made in a different one of the four cities he visits regularly: Six years ago, he bought three water colors by a young Greenwich Village artist, paying a total of $140 for all three. They now have a sale value of $125 apiece. During 1957, my friend was in London, where he found a set of six small, neatly framed 19th Century *gouaches* which he bought for 17 guineas—$51—and for which he was recently offered $250. In 1958, while visiting Paris, he purchased eight early 19th Century prints for the equivalent of $24; two years later, an American dealer offered $150 for the set. Only last year in Venice, my journalist friend saw—and liked—two paintings by the young Italian artist Fioravante Seibezzi and bought them for 30,000 lire—about $50—apiece. Shortly thereafter, Seibezzi had a one-man show that drew critical raves, and the market value of the paintings jumped 300 percent—and is still going up.

My friend has rejected all offers for his acquisitions. Although he is convinced their market values will continue to rise, this is not his reason for refusing to sell. He has the instincts of the true art-loving collector.

"I bought them because I wanted to own them," he explains. "I like them all far too much to sell them for any price anyone is likely to offer."

This astute art investor's experiences serve to underscore the fact that many tourists and people who travel on business often overlook chances to invest wisely in fine art during their travels. They have a habit of shopping for gaudy and frequently costly souvenirs that have little or no value. They fail to realize they could acquire objects of considerable beauty—and of considerable and permanent value—without expending any more effort or money than they spend in buying the trivial.

One man I know served in Japan and Korea with the United States Army. Mildly interested in Oriental art, he used some of his off-duty time looking for a few good pieces to take home. Shunning the main-street stores and tourist-trap bazaars, he poked about in out-of-the-way shops and market places. Spending a total of less than $300, he acquired several pieces for which a San Francisco dealer later offered him $1500.

Another man I know took his wife to Turkey on a holiday in 1956. Instead of buying the tawdry wares traditionally hawked to tourists in many Mediterranean countries, they did their shopping carefully and off the beaten track. They bought some ancient metal castings, figurines and carvings, paying about $650 in all for them. Experts who appraised the items when the couple returned to the United States that same year fixed their immediate sale value at $1400. In the ensuing five years, various factors served to increase this value. By 1961, the art objects for which the couple had paid $650 were worth $2000.

Now, none of these people are art experts. Their knowledge of art is limited to what they have picked up on their own by reading, visiting galleries and exhibitions and browsing in art and antique shops. To them, art collecting is simply a very pleasant extracurricular interest, a hobby if you prefer. They enjoy having objects around them that they consider aesthetically satisfying. They find it makes their lives more pleasurable.

The fundamentals of art collecting are not difficult to master. Obviously, the average person is not financially able to go on a shopping spree for Rembrandts, Fragonards,

Gauguins or other paintings that—when and if available—run into the hundreds of thousands or even millions of dollars.

But even the individual who has only a very few hundred dollars to spend can buy good works of art—objects that are of high quality and that will retain or increase their value.

It stands to reason that the safest way to buy art is to employ an expert to do the buying—or to buy only in the most reputable galleries. But, by so doing, one will be paying the peak current market prices. Also, most people do not have the budgets to buy on the scale such purchasing implies—and many people would rather savor the adventure of shopping for works of art on their own.

However he does it, to buy art wisely, an individual must first make up his mind about what mediums and periods please him the most. He should then learn something—the more the better—about them. There are copies and counterfeits galore on the market—and the only way to distinguish between them and the genuine is by knowing which is which. (Reputable dealers will, of course, almost always permit the prospective buyer the right to have a piece authenticated, or will provide authoritative authentication themselves.)

What to buy? This depends on two factors. The first is the individual's taste—and, if he is to buy wisely, it must be assumed that he has fairly good taste. The second factor is the individual's wallet. Whatever the price range he can afford, the art collector must always strive to buy the best he can within that range. One good item is worth a dozen—or even a hundred—bad ones.

On the one hand, the collector must always remember that artistic value does not necessarily follow the value set by the market place, or vice versa. On the other hand, a collector can appreciate art and revel in its beauty, yet he is entirely justified in wanting to invest his money wisely. It is just as foolish to throw good money away on bad art as it is to throw good money away on anything bad—and only a fool would knowingly overpay for whatever he buys.

Then, to determine whether one really likes a work of art enough to buy it, there is no better rule-of-thumb test than that provided by the classic question he should ask himself: "Can I live with it?" The individual who owns a piece—be it a painting, marble bust, French Renaissance escritoire or whatever—will have to look at it often and long. If he believes an object he contemplates buying will continue to please him over a period of time, then—all other things being equal—he should buy it. If not, he should look for something else. "I buy the things I like—and like the things I buy," is the true collector's guiding philosophy.

Once he has made his purchase, it is up to the individual to decide what he wants to do with it. He has two choices: He can hold it until there is a rise in its market value, sell it and pocket his profit. Or he can keep what he has bought and enjoy it, holding onto it no matter how high the market value goes. If he does this, he can be satisfied that he has invested wisely, for he owns something that has lasting *artistic* value and pays him regular dividends in pleasure even while it unobtrusively continues to increase in monetary value. Either way, buying fine art can be the finest and most satisfying of all investments.

THE
MORALS
OF MONEY

Words such as millionaire, multimillionaire and billionaire carry a magic and compelling ring. Understandably enough, many people are mesmerized by those words, by what they think those words imply—and by the thought of piling up a personal fortune as an end in itself.

These people seem to believe that every millionaire has his millions in ready cash, stored in strongboxes beneath his bed or in a handy wall safe in his library, to hold or squander according to his whim. They also apparently believe that money can buy them everything and solve all their problems.

In the case of a "working" millionaire—a wealthy individual actively engaged in business—nothing could be further from the truth. In the first place, although a businessman may be "worth" many millions of dollars, precious little of his wealth is in fluid, spendable cash. His fortune is invested—tied up— in land, buildings, machinery, equipment, raw materials, finished-product inventories, in all the things which make up his business and keep it in operation.

Certainly, only a minute fraction of any working businessman's fortune is ever available to him as personal cash on hand unless he chooses to go out of business and liquidates his holdings by selling them. But the successful businessman very seldom sells out. He knows that wealth which serves no constructive purpose has no real justification for its existence. It might be said that he views business as a creative art. He uses his money as capital, investing and reinvesting it to create businesses and jobs and produce goods and services.

The successful businessman also knows that wealth does not automatically grant him a year-round, no-limit license for fun-filled frolic. He is well aware that money has the power to do many things *for* people—but he also realizes that money can do many things, bad as well as good, *to* people, their private lives, personalities and moral and intellectual values.

Believe me, wealth is something with which one has to learn to live—and the task is not always as simple as might be imagined. A man who becomes rich finds it necessary to adjust to the idea of being wealthy. He must make certain that he maintains his perspective and his sense of values. He must learn to cope with the special problems his wealth creates, to handle the types of people who are wont to flock around him because he is rich. And even though the successful businessman may not have to worry about his rent or grocery bills, though he may be secure from personal financial want, he is never secure from financial worries. The businessman's wealth derives from the profits made from his business ventures—profits which are dependent upon the efficient operation of those ventures. Consequently, he always has money "problems."

If one of his firms is operating at a loss—as will often happen—he must take immediate steps to remedy the situation. He must find money to finance the expansion and modernization programs of his companies. He must see to it that his companies pay debts promptly. He always has to think—and often has to worry—about these and countless other questions of finance. Take my word for it, a businessman's worries over paying off a $5,000,000 bond issue that has matured are no less great, immediate and personal than those of a $75-a-week clerk who has to meet a $500 note that's falling due!

Once an individual achieves financial success and is identified as a millionaire, he is thenceforth a marked man, and matters only get worse as his wealth increases. If he's seen talking to other businessmen over a restaurant lunch, he is sure to receive a dozen telephone calls a few hours later from people asking him to confirm or deny the reports of projected mergers, stock splits or extra dividend payments which are already making the rounds. Let him attend a social function and dance with a young lady more than once, and the rumors of a "sizzling new romance" which buzz through the ballroom are certain to find their way into the gossip columns. The conversation at the luncheon table may have been concerned solely with hobbies or horse racing. The millionaire's dancing partner may have been his niece or his cousin. But the results are inevitable.

No, despite all the many advantages he enjoys, the wealthy businessman's life is not all champagne and caviar. He must accept the fact that, despite his wealth and position, there *are* drawbacks to being a millionaire. He may be respected or admired for achieving success and wealth, but he must expect that a considerable and vociferous segment of the population will envy and even hate him for it. There are times when he may be praised for what he says or does, but he will be reviled at least as often.

In some ways, a millionaire just can't win. If he spends too freely, he is criticized for being extravagant and ostentatious. If, on the other hand, he lives quietly and thriftily, the same people who would have criticized him for being profligate will call him a miser. If he goes to parties and night clubs, he is labeled a wastrel and doubts are raised about his maturity and sense of responsibility. Let him shun the salons and saloons, and he is promptly tagged as a recluse or misanthrope.

To the auditors and critics of the rich, even the most minor actions loom as matters of major concern. Take tipping, for example. I've found that if I leave a liberal tip in a restaurant, someone is sure to say I'm showing off. If I don't overtip, that same someone will be the first to say that "Paul Getty is a penny pincher." If I talk to reporters word gets around quickly that I'm a publicity hound. If I don't grant interviews, I'm considered "uncooperative" or hostile to the press, and some gossip columnist is certain to write something to the effect that "Paul Getty is strangely uncommunicative these days. Could it be that he's trying to avoid answering certain highly explosive questions?"

Am I complaining? No. Not at all. I'm merely listing some of the things a millionaire has to accept with rueful and resigned good humor.

A wealthy person can obviously buy a plenitude of the material things in life. He can have an extensive wardrobe, automobiles, a fine house, servants—in short, all the *material* appurtenances of luxury living. The extent to which he is able to enjoy these depends on him, and, if he is an active businessman, to a considerable degree on the demands which his business makes upon his time and energies.

I still find that it's often necessary to work 16 and 18 hours a day, and sometimes right around the clock. When I travel, the problems of business are never farther than the nearest telegraph or cable office or telephone. I can't remember a single day of vacation in the last 45 years that was not somehow interrupted by a cable, telegram or telephone call that made me tend to business for at least a few hours. Such work schedules and the need for devoting the majority of my time to building and expanding my businesses have taken a heavy toll of my personal life.

I've been married and divorced five times. I deeply regret these marital failures, but I can understand *why* they were failures. Each one of my former wives is a wonderful woman who did her utmost to make her marriage to me a success. But a woman doesn't feel secure, contented or happy—she doesn't feel as though she is really a wife, or that she really has a husband—when she finds that her husband is thinking of his business interests first and foremost and that she comes next, almost as an afterthought. Five marital failures have also taught me that a happy marriage is another of the countless things in life that no man can buy no matter how many millions he possesses.

Friendship is something else that can't be bought—although there are many who try to sell its counterfeit. I've often said that time is the only reliable gauge by which a wealthy person can measure friendships. I consider myself to be extremely fortunate in having made many real and good friends who have been my friends for years and even decades. They've never tried to profit financially from our friendships. If they have asked me for anything, their requests were reasonable—the kind that good friends are likely to make of each other.

Such is not the case with the familiar type of individual who goes out of his way to become friendly with a wealthy person with premeditated intent to get something for nothing. That "something" may be a job, an inside tip on the stock market, money to start a new business or to shore up an old one that's crumbling, an outright cash gift—or a cash gift that's euphemistically described as a loan.

For example, I have four grown sons. All chose to enter the family business. When each made his decision to do so, he was allowed to start right in—at the bottom of the ladder. My sons served their apprenticeships by serving customers in filling stations owned by companies in which I had large investments. They sold gasoline and lubricating oil, filled batteries, changed tires and did their share of cleaning grease racks and sweeping the premises where they worked. Yet, innumerable casual acquaintances have blandly asked me to do them a "favor" and give *their* sons, or unemployed relatives, executive-level jobs in firms I control. They never seem to understand why I turn them down, and almost always become highly indignant when I do.

Then there are those who ask me for tips which will make them rich overnight—or within a week or two at most. It's useless to tell them I have none to give. The get-rich-quick dreamers won't believe me.

"You damned millionaires are all selfish and unfair!" "You've got secrets for making money, but you won't share them." "You don't want anyone else to get rich!" So go some of the tirades.

Apparently, these individuals believe that modern business is conducted in the dark of the moon by warlocks and sorcerers who chant mystical incantations and draw pentagrams on the floors of board rooms. It doesn't do any good to argue with them. They will not believe that hard work—not tips or secrets—is the key to business success. They don't want to believe it. They want success and wealth served up to them. They don't want to work.

The effect a rich man's money will have on others is often surprising, sometimes barely believable, and by no means always salutary or ennobling. I've said before that a millionaire is a marked man. There are many who consider him an easy mark as well. For instance, I have long been an avid and serious art collector. Through the years, I have been offered bogus Botticellis, counterfeit Corots and fake Fragonards by the carloads.

I recall one man who tried to sell me what he said was a rare 16th Century tapestry, and for "a mere $45,000." When I told him I wasn't interested, he flew into a rage.

"But you've *got* to buy it!" he shouted, thrusting the tapestry at me. "My wife worked months to make it!"

Another enterprising soul informed me that he was breaking up his collection of paintings and showed me several soot-begrimed, tenth-rate canvases in cheap, cracked frames. He had collected the paintings, all right—from scrap heaps and junk shops.

I don't suppose anything illustrates the cupidity and economic ignorance of some people better than the floods of letters by which all reputedly wealthy persons are constantly plagued. I receive up to 3000 letters every month from people who are totally unknown to me. Some are written by women—of all ages and from all walks of life, I gather—who say they've read or heard that I'm extremely rich and currently unmarried.

"You're just the man I've always wanted for a husband . . ." "It's plain to see that you need a wife, and I know I would fill the bill to perfection . . ." "I'll gladly divorce my husband and marry you, if you'll just send me the money to pay the lawyer's fees . . ." These are typical lines taken from some of the marriage-proposal letters sent to me. The ladies often enclose snapshots or *salon* portraits which display greater or lesser quantities of their charms. On occasion, they'll send along entire photo albums. Some of these amorous hopefuls, I might add, hint coyly—or state bluntly—that they're willing to waive the fusty formalities of marriage and overwhelm me with love and companionship provided appropriate financial arrangements are made beforehand.

But the majority of my unwanted mail—about 70 percent, according to a tally made by my secretary—is made up of letters written by people who ask me to send them money. I do not doubt for a moment that some small percentage of these are from individuals who are actually in need. Unfortunately, it is utterly impossible to separate these from the thousands sent by professional panhandlers and chronic beggars. The letters come from practically every country in the world. It would cost vast sums to check the validity of the appeals. Thus, it's necessary to refuse them all.

Like almost all wealthy men—certainly, all with whom I am acquainted—I make my contributions only to organized, legitimate charities. Each and every year, my companies and I contribute sums totaling many hundreds of thousands of dollars to charity. This is the only way one can give money with any degree of assurance that it will be received eventually by deserving persons. I've tried to make this clear in press interviews and public statements, but without avail. Thousands of people who want me to send them money continue to write to me. "You're rich. You'll never miss the money," most of my unbidden correspondents write, as though this explains and justifies everything. Some plead. Others demand. A few even threaten. A surprisingly large number cannily specify that I'm to send them "cash—no checks" because they "don't want the tax authorities to find out about the money." There are even those who demand the sum they request "net —with all taxes paid."

The head of a state medical association once asked me for $250,000—so that he could buy a yacht. "It's not much, considering what I've heard about the size of your fortune," he wrote. This, mind you, was a professional man—a physician who was obviously highly regarded in his community and his state. So, I presume, was the certified public accountant who used his firm's impressive stationery to request $500,000. He'd "discovered a sure-fire system for playing the stock market"— and wanted to play it with my money. "I'll see that you get ten percent of the profits," he promised generously.

Then there was the high-school teacher who wanted a million tax-free dollars so that she could help her relatives, and the banker who wrote that he'd embezzled $100,000 and was certain I would make good his defalcations.

I could cite such examples almost indefinitely. In an average month, the total amount requested by these mail-order mendicants easily exceeds $3,000,000. On one memorable day a short while ago, a *single* mail delivery brought letters asking for a total of no less than $15,000,000!

All this, of course, is but a relatively minor annoyance among the sundry problems that come with wealth. I've mentioned several in this article which serve to make a rich man's life—pleasant and enjoyable as it is in many ways—something less than the carefree idyl so many people picture it to be. Money can do things for people—and it can also do many things *to* them. What money does for or to a particular individual is largely dependent on his moral and intellectual standards, his outlooks and his attitudes toward life.

If he's a businessman, the important consideration is what he *does* with his money. As I have said earlier, the best use he can make of it is to invest it in enterprises which produce more and better goods and services for more people at lower cost. His aim should be to create and operate businesses which contribute their share to the progressive upward movement of the world's economy, and which thus work to make life better for all. Therein lies the justification for wealth, and therefrom does the working businessman derive the greatest sense of satisfaction.

That is what I have tried to do with my money, and those are the aims and goals of the companies in which I have invested. Those are—or should be—the morals of the successful businessman's money.

THE
ART OF
INDIVIDUALITY

The successful executive—the leader, the innovator—is the exceptional man. He is *not* a conformist, except in his adherence to his own ideals and beliefs.

A young business executive I met once might well serve as the prototype for the entire breed of case-hardened conformist "organization men" one finds in ever-increasing numbers in the business world today. His clothes, manners, speech, attitudes—and ideas—were all studied stereotypes. It was obvious that he believed conformity was essential for success in his career, but he complained that he wasn't getting ahead fast enough and asked me if I could offer any advice.

"How can I achieve success and wealth in business?" he asked earnestly. "How can I make a million dollars?"

"I can't give you any sure-fire formulas," I replied, "but I'm certain of one thing. You'll go much further if you stop trying to look and act and think like everyone else on Madison Avenue or Wacker Drive or Wilshire Boulevard. Try being a *non*conformist for a change. Be an individualist—and an individual. You'll be amazed at how much faster you'll 'get ahead.' "

I rather doubt if what I said made much impression on the young man. I fear he was far too dedicated a disciple of that curious present-day hyperorthodoxy, the Cult of Conformity, to heed my heretical counsel. I'm sure he will spend the rest of his life aping and parroting the things he believes, or has been led to believe, are "right" and safe. He'll conform to petty, arbitrary codes and conventions, desperately trying to prove himself stable and reliable—but he will only demonstrate that he is unimaginative, unenterprising and mediocre. The success and wealth for which men such as this yearn will always elude them. They will remain minor executives, shuffled and shunted from one corporate pigeonhole to another, throughout their entire business careers.

I pretend to be neither sage nor savant. Nor would I care to set myself up as an arbiter of anyone's mores or beliefs. But I do think that I know something about business and the business world. In my opinion, no one can possibly achieve any real and lasting success or "get rich" in business by being a conformist. A businessman who wants to be successful cannot afford to imitate others or to squeeze his thoughts and actions into trite and shopworn molds. He must be very much of an individualist who can think and act independently. He must be an original, imaginative, resourceful and entirely self-reliant entrepreneur. If I may be permitted the analogy, he must be a creative artist rather than merely an artisan of business.

The successful businessman's nonconformity is most generally—and most obviously—evident in the manner and methods of his business operations and activities. These will be unorthodox in the sense that they are radically unlike those of his hidebound, less imaginative—and less successful—associates or competitors. Often, his innate impatience with the futility of superficial conventions and dogma of all kinds will manifest itself in varying degrees of personal eccentricity.

Everyone knows about the late John D. Rockefeller, Sr.'s idiosyncratic habit of handing out shiny new dimes wherever he went. Howard Hughes is noted for his penchant for wearing tennis sneakers and open-throated shirts. Bernard Baruch held his most important business conferences on park benches. These are only three among the many multimillionaires who made their fortunes by giving their individualism free rein and who never worried if their nonconformity showed in their private lives.

Now, I would hardly suggest that adoption of some slightly eccentric habit of dress or manner is in itself sufficient to catapult a man to the top of a corporate management pyramid or make him rich overnight. I do, however, steadfastly maintain that few—if any—people who insist on squeezing themselves into stereotyped molds will ever get very far on the road to success.

I find it disheartening that so many young businessmen

today conform blindly and rigidly to patterns they believe some nebulous majority has decreed are prerequisites for approval by society and for success in business. In this, they fall prey to a fundamental fallacy: the notion that the majority is automatically and invariably right. Such is hardly the case. The majority is by no means omniscient just because it is the majority. In fact, I've found that the line which divides majority opinion from mass hysteria is often so fine as to be virtually invisible. This holds as true in business as it does in any other aspect of human activity. That the majority of businessmen think this or that, does not necessarily guarantee the validity of their opinions. The majority often has a tendency to plod slowly or to mill around helplessly. The nonconformist businessman who follows his own counsel, ignoring the cries of the pack, often reaps fantastic rewards. There are classic examples galore—some of the most dramatic ones dating from the Depression.

The Rockefellers began building Rockefeller Center, the largest privately-owned business and entertainment complex in the United States—and possibly the entire world—in 1931, during the depths of the Depression. Most American businessmen considered the project an insane one. They conformed to the prevailing opinion which held that the nation's economy was in ruins and prophesied that the giant skyscrapers would remain untenanted shells for decades. "Rockefeller Center will be the world's biggest White Elephant," they predicted. "The Rockefellers are throwing their money down a bottomless drain." Nonetheless, the Rockefellers went ahead with their plans and built the great Center. They reaped large profits from the project—and proved that they were right, and that the majority was dead wrong.

Conrad Hilton started buying and building hotels when most other hoteliers were eagerly scanning all available horizons for prospective buyers on whom they could unload their properties. There is certainly no need to go into details about nonconformist Conrad Hilton's phenomenal success.

I, myself, began buying stocks during the Depression, when shares were selling at bargain-basement prices and "everyone" believed they would fall even lower.

The conformists were selling out, dumping their stocks on the market for whatever they would bring. Their one thought was to "salvage" what they could before the ultimate economic catastrophe so freely predicted by "the majority" took place.

Nevertheless, I continued to buy stocks. The results? Many shares I bought during the 1930s are now worth a hundred —and more—times what I paid for them. One particular issue in which I purchased sizable blocks has netted me no less than 4500% profit through the years.

No, I'm not boasting nor claiming that I was endowed with any unique powers of economic clairvoyance. There were other businessmen and investors who did the same— and profited accordingly. But we were the exceptions, the nonconformists who refused to be carried along by the wave of dismal pessimism then the vogue with the majority.

The truly successful businessman is essentially a dissenter, a rebel who is seldom if ever satisfied with the status quo. He creates his success and wealth by constantly seeking— and often finding—new and better ways to do and make things.

The list of those who have achieved great success by refusing to accept and follow established patterns is a long one. It spans two centuries of American history and runs the alphabetical gamut from John Jacob Astor to Adolph Zukor. These men relied on those four qualities already enumerated: their own imagination, originality, individualism and initiative. They made good—while the rock-ribbed conformists remained by the wayside.

The conformists simply do not realize that only the least able and efficient among them derive any benefit from the dubious blessings of conformism. The best men are inevitably dragged down to the insipid levels at which the second-raters—the prigs, pedants, precisians and procrastinators—set the pace. The craze for conformity is having its effect on our entire civilization—and, the way I see it, the effect is far from a salubrious one. It isn't a very long step from a conformist society to a regimented society. Although it would take longer to create an Orwellian nightmare through voluntary surrender of individuality—and thus of independence—than through totalitarian edict, the results would be very much the same. In some respects, a society in which the members reach a universal level in which they are anonymous drones by choice is even more frightening than one in which they are forced to be so against their will. When human beings relinquish their individuality and identity of their own volition, they are also relinquishing their claim to being human.

In business, the mystique of conformity is sapping the dynamic individualism that is the most priceless quality an executive or businessman can possibly possess. It has produced the lifeless, cardboard-cutout figure of the organization man who tries vainly to hide his fears, lack of confidence and incompetence behind the stylized façades of conformity.

The conformist is not born. He is made. I believe the brainwashing process begins in the schools and colleges. Many teachers and professors seem hell-bent on imbuing their students with a desire to achieve "security" above all—and at all costs. Beyond this, high school and university curricula are frequently designed to turn out nothing but "specialists" with circumscribed knowledge and interests. The theory seems to be that accountants should only be accountants, traffic managers should only be traffic managers, and so on ad nauseam. There doesn't appear to be much effort made to produce young men who have a grasp of the over-all business picture and who will assume the responsibilities of leadership. Countless otherwise intelligent young men leave the universities where they have received overspecialized educations and then disappear into one of the administrative rabbit warrens of our overorganized corporations.

To be sure, there are many other pressures that force the young man of today to be a conformist. He is bombarded from all sides by arguments that he must tailor himself, literally and figuratively, to fit the current clean-cut image, which means that he must be just like everyone else. He does not understand that the arguments are those of the almost-weres and never-will-bes who want him as company to share the misery of their frustrations and failures. Heaven help the man who dares to be different in thought or action. Any deviation from the mediocre norm, he is told, will brand him a Bohemian or a Bolshevik, a crank or a crackpot—a man who is unpredictable and thus unreliable.

This, of course, is sheer nonsense. Any man who allows his individuality to assert itself constructively will soon rise to the top. He will be the man who is most likely to succeed. But the brainwashing continues throughout many a man's career. The women of his life frequently do their part to keep him in his conformist's strait jacket. Mothers, fiancées and wives are particularly prone to be arch-conservatives who consider a weekly paycheck a bird in hand to be guarded, cherished and protected—and never mind what valuable *rara avis* may be nesting in the nearby bushes. Wives have a habit of raising harrowing spectres to deter a husband who might wish to risk his safe, secure job and seek fulfillment and wealth via imaginative and enterprising action. "You've got a good future with the Totter and Plod Company," they wail. "Don't risk it by doing anything rash. Remember all the bills and payments we have to meet—and we simply *must* get a new car this year!"

Consequently, the full-flowering conformist organization man takes the 8:36 train every weekday morning and hopes that in a few years he'll be moved far enough up the ladder so that he can ride the 9:03 with the middle-bracket executives. The businessman conformist is the Caspar Milquetoast of the present era. His future is not very bright. His conformist's rut will grow ever deeper until, at last, it becomes the grave for the hopes, ambitions and chances he might have once had for achieving wealth and success. The confirmed organization man spends his business career bogged down in a morass of procedural rules, multi-copy memoranda and endless committee meetings in which he and the men who are his carbon copies come up with hackneyed answers to whatever problems are placed before them. He worries and frets about things that are trivial and superficial—even unto wearing what someone tells him is the "proper" garb for an executive in his salary bracket and to buying his split-level house in what some canny realtor convinces him is an "executives' subdivision."

Such a man defeats his own purpose. He remains a second-string player on what he somewhat sophomorically likes to call "the team," instead of becoming the captain or star player. He misses the limitless opportunities which today present themselves to the imaginative individualist. But he really doesn't care. "I want security," he declares. "I want to know that my job is safe and that I'll get my regular raises in salary, vacations with pay and a good pension when I retire." This, unhappily, seems to sum up too many young men's ambitions. It is a confession of weakness and cowardice.

The Art of Individuality

There is a dearth of young executives who are willing to stick their necks out, to assert themselves and fight for what they think is right and best even if they have to pound on the corporation president's desk to make their point.

True, an executive who crosses swords with his superiors may sometimes risk his job in the process, but a firm that will fire a man merely because he has the courage of his convictions is not one for which a really good executive would care to work in the first place. And, if he is a good executive, he will quickly get a better job in the event he *is* fired—you may be sure of that. You can also be sure that the conformist who never dares vary from the norm will stay in the lower—or at best middle—echelons in any firm for which he works. He will not reach the top or get rich by merely seeking to second-guess his superiors. The man who will win success is the man who is markedly different from the others around him. He has new ideas and can visualize fresh approaches to problems. He has the ability—and the will—to think and act on his own, not caring if he is damned or derided by "the majority" for his nonconformist ideas and actions.

The men who will make their marks in commerce, industry and finance are the ones with freewheeling imaginations and strong, highly individualistic personalities. Such men may not care whether their hair is crewcut or in a pompadour, and they may prefer chess to golf—but they will see and seize the opportunities around them. Their minds unfettered by the stultifying mystiques of organization-man conformity, they will be the ones to devise new concepts by means of which production and sales may be increased. They will develop new products and cut costs—to increase profits and build their own fortunes. These economic free-thinkers are the individuals who create new businesses and revitalize and expand old ones. They rely on their own judgment rather than on surveys, studies and committee meetings. They refer to no manuals of procedural rules, for they know that every business situation is different from the next and that no thousand volumes could ever contain enough rules to cover all contingencies.

The successful businessman is no narrow specialist. He knows and understands all aspects of his business. He can spot a production bottleneck as quickly as he can an accounting error, rectify a weakness in a sales campaign as easily as a flaw in personnel procurement methods. The successful businessman is a leader—who solicits opinion and advice from his subordinates, but makes the final decisions, gives the orders and assumes the responsibility for whatever happens. I've said it before, and I say it again: There is a fantastic demand for such men in business today—both as top executives and as owners and operators of their own businesses. There is ample room for them in all categories of business endeavor.

The resourceful and aggressive man who wants to get rich will find the field wide open, provided he is willing to heed and act upon his imagination, relying on his own abilities and judgment rather than conforming to patterns and practices established by others.

The nonconformist—the leader and originator—has an excellent chance to make his fortune in the business world. He can wear a green toga instead of a gray-flannel suit, drink yak's milk rather than martinis, drive a Kibitka instead of a Cadillac and vote the straight Vegetarian Ticket—and none of it will make the slightest difference. Ability and achievement are bona fides no one dares question, no matter how unconventional the man who presents them.

A
SENSE OF
VALUES

To be truly rich, regardless of his fortune or lack of it, a man must live by his own values. If those values are not personally meaningful, then no amount of money gained can hide the emptiness of a life without them.

I have known entirely too many people who spend their lives trying to be what others want them to be and doing what others expect them to do. They force themselves into patterns of behavior which have been established for—and by—people with personalities entirely different from their own. Seeking to conform to those patterns, they dissolve into grotesque, blurred mirror images as they obliterate their individuality to imitate others. Rootless, dissatisfied, they strive frantically—and most often vainly—to find their own identities within the constricting limits of an existence alien to their natures, instincts and innate desires.

"I wanted to be a writer. My father refused to hear of it and insisted I go to law school and become an attorney. I make a good living now, but I'm bored and restless . . ."

"I'd like to sell my business and buy a ranch somewhere, but my wife won't let me because she's afraid it would mean a loss of income and prestige . . ."

"There's nothing I hate more than suburban living. I'd much rather have an apartment in the city, but all the other executives in my firm have homes in the suburbs . . ."

"I feel trapped, as though I'm caught up in a pointless rat race. I really don't like or enjoy my work, but I don't know what else I could do and still make as much money as I'm making now . . ."

I've heard such statements as these made with ever-increasing frequency in recent years. Essentially, they are expressions of personal discontent—and even defeat—but they also reflect a constantly growing social illness of our time.

The post-World War One period was said to have produced a confused, insecure and disillusioned Lost Generation. There is, tragically enough, ample evidence to indicate that the post-World War Two era produced a generation which has, in large part, lost its sense of perspective and purpose. It is a generation whose members are prone to substitute flimsy dollars-and-cents price tags for scales of lasting values and who meekly surrender their individuality and even their integrity as human beings. A glaringly obvious manifestation of this can be found in the social phenomenon of status seeking, which has become so widespread and prevalent that it looms as one of the principle motivating forces behind our contemporary social behavior patterns.

Now, I agree that the desire of human beings to rise above the mass and to gain the respect of their fellow men is a basic one. Within certain broad limits and subject to certain self-evident reservations, it is a constructive and salutary motivation. The desire to excel has impelled countless individuals to make important contributions to the progress of civilization. But, as more than one observer has noted, the rationale of today's status seeking and the directions it takes are neither constructive nor healthy.

To my way of thinking, status may be defined as a form of recognition an individual's peers award him for above-average contributions to society. It is something that must be earned, a reward for accomplishment that is awarded at a degree proportionate to the value or importance of what the individual contributes toward the common good. Nowadays, however, the tendency is to equate status almost automatically—and all but exclusively—with financial success. And, it seems that the achievement of status not only is, per se, considered an end unto itself, but that for many it has become the sole motivation and the only worthwhile goal.

Vast numbers of people have apparently convinced themselves that the amassing of money and the material things it can buy alone signifies achievement, connotes success and confers status. They pile up money and the material possessions which they believe are solid proofs rather than frail symbols of ability, achievement and success. They accept as manifest truth the shoddy theory that they can gain social position and the respect of others only by outearning and outbuying those around them. They have no interest in building anything but their own bank balances; they are not concerned with values, but only with the dollars-and-cents prices they pay for their possessions.

I've encountered more concrete examples of this distorted viewpoint than I'd care to count. Quite typical of them was my recent experience with a businessman who paid me a visit in London, arriving with a letter of introduction from a mutual acquaintance in New York. After spending more than two hours boasting about how much money he'd made in the last few years, my visitor informed me that he was on his way to France, where he intended to buy some paintings.

"I've heard that you're quite an art collector," he said. "I thought you could help me out by giving me the names and addresses of some reliable art galleries or dealers from whom I could do my buying."

"Are you interested in paintings from any special period or of any particular school?" I inquired. "Or are you looking for works by some particular artist?"

"It doesn't make any difference to me," the man shrugged impatiently. "I wouldn't know one from another in any case. I just have to buy some paintings—and I have to spend at least $100,000 for them."

"Why can't you spend less than that?" I asked, puzzled that anyone would set an arbitrary minimum rather than a maximum on what he wanted to spend.

"Oh, it's one of those things," came the straight-faced explanation. "My partner was over here a couple of months ago and he paid $75,000 for some pictures. I figure that to make any kind of an impression back home, I've got to top him by at least $25,000 . . ."

It is easy to see how this man judges values. I strongly suspect that it is also a safe bet that whatever he has done in life, his motives were always just as shallow and trivial as his purely status-seeking reasons for wanting to buy paintings. Unfortunately, there are many people like him. In my opinion, it would be difficult to find justification for their wealth; I do not believe they really earn—or, for that matter, deserve—their money.

I am a stubborn advocate of enlightened free-enterprise Capitalism and the last person in the world to question anyone's fundamental right to achieve financial success. I contend that a person who possesses the imagination and ability to "get rich" and goes about his money-making activities legitimately should be allowed every opportunity to do so. On the other hand, I firmly believe that an individual who seeks financial success should be motivated by much more than merely a desire to amass a personal fortune.

My own father, as I have said, was poor—very poor—in his youth, and although he made a great deal of money during his lifetime, he did not make it with any intention of caching it away for his own exclusive benefit. He knew the value of money and had very definite ideas about its uses. My father considered his wealth primarily as capital, to be invested for the direct benefit of his employees, associates, stockholders, customers and their families.

His attitude toward his wealth was governed by a maxim he took from Sir Francis Bacon: "No man's fortune can be an end worthy of his being." He loved the challenge of business, but the incentive was not to pile up money, but rather to accomplish something lasting. I doubt seriously if his total personal and family expenditures ever exceeded $30,000 a year—yet, he was probably one of the first businessmen to build swimming pools and provide other recreational facilities for his employees.

I learned from my father that the astute, progressive and truly successful businessman does not think of his work primarily in terms of profits. The money value of my holdings in the companies I own or control has been estimated in the hundreds of millions of dollars. But this is a paper fortune and it is still a means and not an end. Only an infinitesimal part of my fortune is held by me in cash. My wealth is represented by machinery, oil wells, pipelines, tankers, refineries, factory and office buildings—by all the myriad assets of the companies in which I have invested my capital. And those companies are continuing to produce goods and perform services—and to grow and expand. Thus, my wealth is continuing to perform useful, creative work. These are the worth-while ends to which wealth is a means, and which give money its real value.

I do not measure my success in terms of dollars and cents. I measure it in terms of the jobs and the productivity my labors and my wealth—invested and reinvested as capital in my various business enterprises—have made possible. I doubt very seriously if I could have reached anywhere near the level of success that I have reached if I'd employed any other yardsticks to gauge my progress during my career.

I've found that, to establish his identity, to feel that he is a fully participating member of society, an individual must have purpose and feel that what he does has some enduring value well beyond the limits of his own personal interests. In order to achieve any contentment in life, he must derive genuine satisfaction and an equally genuine sense of accomplishment from his work. These are considerations at least as important as the size of the income he receives from his job, profession or business.

By no means am I suggesting that a vow of poverty—or anything even remotely approaching it—will provide an individual with a shortcut to ecstatic bliss. There is very little room for the wandering mendicant and his begging-bowl in our civilization. Human beings have progressed well beyond the stage where they can be satisfied with their lot while living on a diet of black bread and boiled cabbage. They must have decent living standards—all the necessities and many of the luxuries of life—if they are to be even moderately content. For these things, they must earn money.

This does not, however, change the fact that there are many ways of gauging values besides placing them on a monetary scale. A badly written, banal contemporary novel may sell for five dollars a copy, while a great literary classic may be purchased in a paperback edition for 50 cents. Certainly the latter has infinitely greater real *value* than the former, regardless of the tremendous disparity in their prices. By the same token, there are many kinds of success other than purely financial success. I hold that an individual's standing in society should be judged by criteria other than merely his income, accumulated monetary wealth or the number and money value of his material possessions.

Past and present, there are uncounted examples of individuals who made priceless contributions to civilization, but who realized little or no monetary rewards from what they did. Innumerable great philosophers, scientists, artists and musicians were poor men all their lives. Mozart, Beethoven, Modigliani and Gauguin—among others of comparable stature—died poverty-stricken. No one on earth could possibly estimate the value of the contributions made to mankind by such men as the late Dr. Albert Schweitzer or the late Dr. Thomas Dooley; yet, it's highly doubtful if either of them ever enjoyed a personal income as large as that earned by the average department-store buyer.

The architect who designs a breathtakingly beautiful building is often a poor man compared to the tenants who will occupy it. The engineer who builds a dam may well earn less from his labors than the landowner whose acres are irrigated by water from the dam. The architect and engineer have created and built; their success is no less great because they did not earn fortunes from their work.

Also largely overlooked in this age of treadmill scrambling for money and status is the fact that there are many forms of wealth other than financial wealth. One of the most genuinely contented men I've ever known was my cousin, Hal Seymour. Hal and I grew up together; we were always close friends and for long periods we were constant companions. Hal cared very little for money. Content to earn enough for his own needs, he good-naturedly turned down every opportunity I offered him for earning more. Working here and there—he was a topflight oil driller, photographer, miner, a master of many trades—he never had much money. But he managed to satisfy his desires to go many places and do many things—and he always enjoyed himself thoroughly with the armies of friends he made wherever he went. His aim in life was always to do whatever he attempted well. He realized this aim; he always gave more than he took.

Hal considered himself to be very wealthy in personal freedom. He was always able to do the things he wanted to do, and always had the time in which to do them. He seldom missed a chance to remind me that, in these regards, I was much poorer than he. Before his death a few years ago, he frequently wrote me letters which opened with the wryly humorous but meaningful salutation: "To the Richest Man in the World from the Wealthiest . . ."

I'll have to admit that I envied Hal his abundance of time —which is one of the forms of wealth that people tend to disregard these days. Rich as I may be from a material standpoint, I've long felt that I'm very poor, indeed, in time. For decades, my business affairs have made extremely heavy inroads on my time, leaving me very little I could use as I pleased. There are books that I have wanted to read—and books I have wanted to write. I've always yearned to travel to remote parts of the globe which I've never seen; one of my greatest unfulfilled ambitions has been to go on a long, leisurely safari in Africa.

Money has not been a bar to the realization of these desires; insofar as money is concerned, I could have easily afforded to do any of these things for many years. The blunt and simple truth is that I've never been able to do them because I could never afford the time. It's paradoxical but true that the so-called captains of industry frequently have less time for indulging their personal desires than their rear-rank privates. This applies to little things as well as big ones.

It is not my intent to imply that I am in any way dissatisfied with my lot in life. Indeed, I would be more than ungrateful for the good fortune and advantages I've enjoyed if I were anything less than happy. Moreover, I am very gratified that I have managed to accomplish most of the goals I set for myself when I began my business career.

The point I'm trying to make is that each individual has to establish his own standards of values, and that these are largely subjective. They are based on what the individual considers most important to him and what he is willing to give for a certain thing or in order to achieve a certain aim.

Old—but true—are the bromides that you can't have everything and that you can't get something for nothing. An individual always has to give—or give up—something in order to have or get something else. Whether he's willing to make the exchange or not is entirely up to him and his own sense of values.

Acknowledging all this, I nevertheless believe that there are certain values which, if not absolute in the strict sense of the word, are surely basic and can be said to be generally valid. I never cease to be amazed by the casual and even callous manner in which sizable segments of our population ignore these fundamental values.

It is estimated that more than 120,000 Americans take their

own lives each year. This figure includes cases which are officially recorded as suicides and the cases of those who do away with themselves, but whose deaths, for one reason or another, are not recorded officially as such. A significant portion of these 120,000 annual tragedies are classed as "economic suicides."

According to Dr. Thomas P. Malone, head of the Atlanta, Georgia, Psychiatric Clinic, an acknowledged authority on the macabre subject: "At least 30 to 40 percent of so-called economic suicides occur when a man is successful, not when he is failing. When a man has achieved the peak of success, often he has nothing left to scramble for."

I'm no psychiatrist, but it seems to me that anyone who takes his own life because he has achieved success and has "nothing left to scramble for" never had any worthwhile motives to scramble for in the first place. The goals he sought— and achieved—were meaningless. When he realized this he also realized that what he had actually achieved was not success but pathetic failure.

In a report in the *Journal of the American Medical Association*, Drs. Richard E. and Katherine K. Gordon revealed the results of an intensive study they made of families living in a typical contemporary status-seekers' suburban community. They determined that the diseases which stem primarily from emotional stresses—notably ulcers, coronary thrombosis, hypertension and hypertensive cardiovascular disease—were markedly more prevalent there than in communities in which status seeking was not such a dominant social factor. Anyone who has encountered specimens of the ulcer-ridden, tranquilizer-devouring and status-seeking Organization Man and their nervously shrill-voiced, apprehensive wives will hardly be surprised by this revelation.

I am unable to see that the achievement of any degree of social status is worth the price of a man's life or the destruction of his or his family's health. Assuredly, there is something very wrong basically when human beings are willing to sell their lives and their health so cheaply. Nor am I able to see that money or the dubious benefits conferred by the attainment of what passes for status are worth the price of one's individuality and personal integrity. I am apparently in the minority. It is becoming increasingly apparent that it's no longer fashionable to pay much heed to these considerations. Their value has been swept aside in the pell-mell rush to conform to what is regarded as the majority view—which regards the accumulation of money and material things and the gaining of status as the approved goals and places no ceiling on the price which can be paid for achieving them.

I consider it one of the major tragedies of our civilization that people have come to regard it virtually mandatory to imitate in order to win the social acceptance of their fellows. The end result of this can only be to reduce even the most brilliant individuals to a sterile cipher.

Toady and lickspittle are nasty words. The average man would probably be inclined to use his fists on anyone who called him either. Yet, countless men will lower themselves to such absurd devices as wearing bow ties because their employers wear them, cutting their hair the way their superiors do, or buying their homes where the other executives buy theirs. They ape and echo the ideas, views and actions of those they seek to impress, proving nothing but that they are servile toadies. Imitation may be the most sincere form of flattery— but it *is* imitation, and flattery is nothing more than a pat on the head from someone who knows he deserves a kick in the behind.

I once obtained control of a company and was immediately —and far from favorably—impressed by the fawning attitude of the majority of the firm's executives. Most were obsequious yes-men feverishly trying to please the new boss so that they could further their own narrow ambitions. Wanting to see just how far they were willing to go, I called a special management meeting. At the meeting, I proposed a wholly impractical and ruinous scheme which, if implemented, would have quickly bankrupted the firm.

Of the nine executives present, six instantly expressed their approval of my "plans." Three of these men went to the extreme of modestly hinting that they'd been "thinking along similar lines"—something I could well believe from having studied the firm's profit-and-loss statements. Two very junior executives remained glumly and disapprovingly silent. Only one man in the group had the temerity to stand up and point out the flaws in my proposal.

Needless to say, the company soon had some new faces in

its executive offices. The three dissidents remained; all are still associated with my companies and, I might add, are now in the upper income brackets.

It has always been my contention that an individual who can be relied upon to be himself and to be honest unto himself can be relied upon in every other way. He places value—not a price—on himself and his principles. And that, in the final analysis, is the measure of anyone's sense of values—and of the true worth of any man.